in his own words

Elton John

W9-DHY-823

Susan Black

OMNIBUS PRESS
LONDON · NEW YORK · PARIS · SYDNEY

Copyright © 1993 Omnibus Press
(A Division of Book Sales Limited)

Edited by Chris Charlesworth
Cover & Book designed by Michael Bell Design
Picture research by David Brolan

ISBN: 0.7119.3213.1
Order No: OP 47157

All rights reserved. No part of this book may be reproduced in any form or by any electronic or
mechanical means, including information storage or retrieval systems, without permission in writing
from the publisher, except by a reviewer who may quote brief passages.

Exclusive distributors:
Book Sales Limited,
8/9 Frith Street,
London W1V 5TZ, UK.

Music Sales Corporation,
225 Park Avenue South,
New York, NY 10003, USA.

Music Sales Pty Ltd,
120 Rothschild Avenue,
Rosebery, NSW 2018, Australia.

To the Music Trade only:
Music Sales Limited,
8/9 Frith Street,
London W1V 5TZ, UK.

Photo credits:
Richie Aaron/Redferns: 111t; Adrian Boot/Retna: 82; Lester Cohen: 90b;
Dave Ellis/Redferns: 42t; Famous: 111b; Bob Gruen/Pictorial Press: 13, 26t, 53t, 106t;
Bob King/Redferns: 72t; Phil Loftus/Retna: 83; London Features International: back cover (x2), 4,
8t&b, 9, 17, 18, 20, 21t, 23, 26b, 27, 28, 32, 33, 34, 37t&b, 39, 40 (inset), 42b, 43, 44t, 46, 47t&b,
48, 50t&b, 53b, 54, 55, 56, 60, 61b, 62t&b, 63, 64, 65, 66t&b, 69, 70t&b, 71, 73, 76, 81, 84t&b,
85, 86/87, 89, 90t, 91, 93, 95t&c, 98, 102, 103t&b, 104, 110; Janet Macoska/Retna: 57;
Kevin Mazur/Retna: 68; Pictorial Press: 6, 14, 16, 30, 72b, 92; Barry Plummer: 12, 15, 22, 31, 35,
36, 38, 40, 44b, 45, 49, 58, 59, 74, 75, 77, 80t, 88, 96, 101, 106b, 107, 108;
Michael Putland/Retna: 7, 29, 51, 52, 61t, 67, 80b, 94, 97, 99, 100, 112;
David Redfern/Redferns: 21b; Peter Sanders/Redferns: 24/25; Barrie Wentzell/Pictorial Press: 78;
Val Wilmer/Redferns: 10; Vinnie Zuffante/Pictorial Press: 109.

Printed and bound in Great Britain by Scotprint Limited, Musselburgh, Scotland.

Every effort has been made to trace the copyright holders of the photographs in this book but one or
two were unreachable. We would be grateful if the photographers concerned would contact us.

A catalogue record for this book is available from the British Library.

Introduction

Elton John has rarely been at a loss for words. Neither has the UK's most durable singer/songwriter shied away from controversy, all of which makes a collection of his quotes fascinating both to compile and read.

As his career gained momentum in the early Seventies Elton bubbled over with enthusiasm for rock and pop music and the music industry in general. Like a child given free rein in a toy shop, he rarely refused an interview, whether it was with the then influential and all important music press or less important local media, and he always had a considered but frank opinion on the state of his career, the state of rock or whatever it was that was on his mind at the time, musical or otherwise. He became a favourite with interviewers, and while he could never be accused of manipulating the media as skilfully as Bob Dylan or David Bowie, he was always good for a quote and never afraid to speak his mind.

Perhaps the most celebrated interview that Elton ever gave was with Rolling Stone magazine in 1976, when he spoke on the record about his bisexuality for the first time. This was not a calculated move to shock - as Bowie's similar 'admission' had been in 1972 - but a brave and genuine response to a line of questioning he hadn't encountered before, and his honest response reflected the sense of decency which has been a consistent thread throughout his long relationship with the press.

At times Elton has shied away from talking to the media, feeling - quite rightly - that overexposure might harm his credibility. He has also been misquoted and there have been occasions when things he has said off the record have found their way into print, a dilemma all loquacious celebrities face from time to time. This perhaps explains why he clammed up during the late Seventies and Eighties - the period when he backed away from music and devoted much of his time and energy to Watford Football Club - and why so many of the quotes in this book come from the first flush of his career.

More recently, however, Elton has adopted the not unfashionable 'confessional' style of interview in which he publicly acknowledges assorted bad habits of the drug and drink variety and indiscretions, emotional turmoil and illnesses arising from them. Like so many of his contemporaries, he became addicted, suffered and has now decided to come clean, both physically and mentally, and feels the need to talk about what happened, probably in the hope that others will learn from his mistakes.

Elton John now ranks among the elder statesmen of British rock, and his knowledge and experience in pop music and the music industry are as profound as any of his peers. Much of that knowledge and experience is communicated in the pages that follow.

Susan Black, 1993

Early Days

Elton was born Reg Dwight in Pinner on March 25, 1947...
When I was four, I had a mass of bubbly hair. I looked like Shirley
Temple. My piano idols were Charlie Kunz, who'd been famous in
Britain for years, and Winifred Atwell, the West Indian who'd settled
in Britain and was great at playing anything from the classics to pop.
'The Skater's Waltz' became my first main party piece.

When I was a kid I was always being told not to do things.
Until my parents got divorced I was suppressed by and petrified
of my father... I was never allowed to do this, that or the other.
My father wasn't the slightest bit interested in me and he was a snob.
I dreaded it when he came home.

My father didn't want me to get into music and I could never
understand that because he'd been a trumpeter in a band. I mean,
he did influence me... used to play me his George Shearing records.
A four-year-old listening to George Shearing is a bit off...
I was more into Guy Mitchell.

His parents soon separated...
I was terribly bitter about *(the divorce)* at the time. I see my dad
now sometimes and I feel really sorry that we didn't get closer.
He has a new family that he loves. I just wish he could have loved
me like that too. (1975)

As a child I desperately wanted brothers and sisters. But my father
was against the idea. *(Childhood)* was miserable. I lost touch with my
father. There was a wide rift between us. My father seemed to resent
me. Maybe it was a mistake. I don't know... I feel sorry for my father
in a way that we didn't ever get close and never had a man to
man chat. What has gone in the past has gone.

I was probably a good enough scholar to go to university, but
I never tried more than 30 per cent. I was always into pop music or
football and I just squeezed through my exams. I was very lazy. (1972)

Elton's mother Sheila always encouraged his love of music...
My parents always forced me to play. If I was at a wedding, for
example, they'd say 'Come on! Give us a song!'

I was brought up on my parents' pile of 78s, people like Guy
Mitchell, Frankie Laine, Rosemary Clooney, Kay Starr, Billy May...
all the early Fifties stuff. My first favourite of all was Winifred
Atwell... I was knocked out by her.

Elton with Little Richard.

My mother came home one afternoon with two discs. She said she never heard anything like them and thought they were fantastic. When I heard them, I agreed. They were Elvis's 'Heartbreak Hotel' and Bill Haley's 'ABC Boogie'. I'll never forget that: one was on Brunswick and the other on HMV. I really freaked when I heard them and I went on from there. The first thing I read about Elvis was in a barber's shop and I couldn't believe it.

I began wearing glasses when I was 13 to copy Buddy Holly. After 18 months I found I couldn't see without them. I looked terrible *(as a young performer)*, a fatty with glasses and with a terrible inferiority complex. It took me years to lose it. I never liked night clubs.

Every day I used to come home from school and play until somebody was able to make me stop. Eventually my mother and father became nervous wrecks and we had complaints from the neighbours.

I didn't have any formal training *(at the piano)* at first. I just sat down and I could play. I started picking out tunes and went on like that for about three years, then my parents suggested I should take lessons and I stuck with them until I won a Scholarship to the Royal Academy of Music. But I never enjoyed the lessons. It was a bore, and I didn't like practising. (1972)

I used to get a certain amount of pocket money each week and I remember buying a Little Richard record, 'She's Got It' and 'The Girl Can't Help It', and my mother wouldn't let me play it. She liked rock but not Little Richard, and I was really annoyed because it was my favourite record. I was really star struck. Pop music was my whole life.

I've been collecting records for years. I've got a lot of original American records difficult to find in England – about 1,400 singles, 300 LPs and 100 EPs. Some are real collector's items. Bernie's *(Taupin)* got about 90 LPs too and we don't know where to put them all. (1969)

*Elton's first paid work as a musician was as a pub pianist at the
Northwood Hills Hotel in Pinner...*
When I first started I was a real duff.

I first faced an audience in 1964. I was just 16. I sang and played
piano in the public bar of the Northwood Hills Hotel every Friday,
Saturday and Sunday for a whole year. I was paid a pound a night,
but I used to have a box passed around at the end of the evening.
I had to play an old upright piano that was out of tune and I sang
through a little amplifier.

I was still a schoolboy of 16 and played the bar piano every
Friday, Saturday and Sunday. I was there a year, singing Jim Reeves
and Cliff Richard songs – anything that was popular. But I also used
to play things like 'Roll Out The Barrel' and 'When Irish Eyes Are
Smilin'', otherwise you'd get a pint of beer slung over you.
Al Jolson songs were also very popular.

When I first started nobody used to go into the public bar but
eventually people started to come in and after a while it was packed
out every weekend. At one stage I used to earn £25 a week. It was
great training because I played on an old upright piano that was
out of tune and there were a couple of times when I had to dive out
of the window when really bad fights broke out. Anyway, I saved
up enough money to buy a Hohner electric piano and amplifier.
Pub entertaining is the finest ground for teaching you discipline.

I used to take my box around. People would put donations in it.
I was making a fortune compared to the rest of the kids. I was getting
about £35 a week.

I landed myself a job as a junior in Mills Music – a publishing firm
in London's Tin Pan Alley. It was what I wanted. I was bored with
school and happy to leave, though my music teacher protested
at my decision.

So far as education and learning the piano went, I never achieved
what I could have done. But that was because I knew I wanted
something else.

Bluesology

*In 1961 Elton joined the band that would become Bluesology and who
often backed visiting US soul singers…*
At primary school I was brilliant. At grammar school I was good…
at getting out of things, like the school choir in the lunch break.
I used to go off and play football. I was going to take A-levels but
I got bored with school so I left and got a job as a tea boy in a music
publishing office, playing with a group in the evenings.

I met this guy Stuart Brown, a friend of my cousin, who played
the guitar. I was very fat and when I said I played the piano he laughed
helplessly. I showed him. I did my Jerry Lee Lewis bit and he stopped
laughing. We got a band together that played in Boy Scout huts.

At first it was all a hobby. We had no amplifiers. It all faded out
after a few months. It was just a pastime. Then a couple of years later
I ran into him again and he suggested that we put another band
together so we did. That was Bluesology.

We started with a four-piece and then we decided to add brass
so we put an ad in the paper and got a tenor sax player and trumpeter
who were much better musicians than the rest of us.

As a semi-pro group we got quite a bit of work and we were
ambitious and dedicated to the point of taking the plunge and adding
a trumpet and a saxophone which was partly because of the emergence
of Otis Redding style arrangements. Thinking we were a cut above
the average club band, we concentrated on rather more obscure
material, things like 'Times Are Getting Tougher Than Tough'
by Jimmy Witherspoon.

Our first job was backing Wilson Pickett – can you imagine how
we felt? He was such an important figure in the music we were playing,
and here we were about to tour as his band! Well, we went to rehearse
with his guitarist – but he didn't like our drummer, and he didn't
particularly like the rest of us either, so that tour was blown out, and
we were very brought down.

Bluesology would never let me sing, so I really only started when
we were doing our first demos, and my voice improved – I hope –
as I did more and more.

I didn't really want to be lead singer of Bluesology. I just wanted
to do backing vocals… 'Ooos' and 'Ahhhs'. But I wasn't really even
allowed to do that.

We played the Cavern Club in Liverpool twice and it was definitely one of the worst places for getting your gear nicked, so bad we had to keep someone posted all the time. And the overflow from the men's toilets was disgusting.

I'm quite large now, but then I was 14 stone – and I was stuck behind a Vox Continental when what I really wanted to do was sing.

I remember we once did four gigs in a day, and we never thought anything of it. That was with Billy Stewart, who was a great guy. I shudder to think of that now, and we didn't even have a roadie then. Groups today, they don't know how lucky they are.

Billy Stewart was the greatest. Billy got us together so well. He was absolutely brilliant on stage... incredible. His timing, showmanship and voice were just great.

Sometimes we did four gigs in one day, with someone like Billy Stewart. We did the US Serviceman's Club at Douglas House, Lancaster Gate, at around four in the afternoon, then we did the Ritz and the Plaza Ballroom in Birmingham and then we finished off by playing the Cue Club in Paddington at round six in the morning. If playing four gigs wasn't bad enough, we had to load up, unload and set up our own equipment at each gig.

In 1966 Bluesology became the permanent back-up unit for Long John Baldry…
Baldry's first move was to get Stuart to drop his guitar and

Long John Baldry.

concentrate entirely on vocals, to bring in another singer and to turn it into a three singers up front type of band. We got two new brass players and it wasn't a bad little band at that stage.

I remember doing an audition with Marsha *(Hunt)* which was just hysterical... the only thing she knew was 'Love Is A Many Splendoured Thing', and she didn't know what key she wanted so she sang unaccompanied. Some in the band said she was awful but Baldry said no, she looks all right. She was knocked out, and we started doing this big soul package thing.

He *(Baldry)* took pills to get thin and they worked, they also tended to make him aggressive, and short-tempered.

The saddest gig we ever did was the Ink Spots tour. They were old guys and should've been doing cabaret to audiences who had heard of them, but they were put out on the ballroom circuit and all the kids would disappear back to the bar as soon as they started singing. That Christmas, we were doing three gigs a night for a while – the

Sheffield Cavendish, Tito's in Stockton and South Shields Latino; we were the night club entertainment to help the food go down nicely.

We started playing big ballrooms. The high spot of our act was when Baldry used to sing his hit ('When The Heartaches Begin') to a backing tape that we had to mime to. As Baldry's style changed towards the soft ballady stuff, we moved into cabaret and it was really beginning to bring me down. We were the night club entertainment to help the food go down nicely. I began looking through the papers to try and find a job. I didn't care what it was, working in a record shop... anything...

I just wanted to be on the stage to show people what I could do, and that's why I got very brought down by Bluesology, because I was just nothing. There's so many people going round in bands who are afraid to take the plunge or don't get the chance. They really want to break out but they daren't; the only reason I did was because I was desperate and miserable that I just had to.

I looked terrible, it was a good band, good musicians, but everybody just wanted their forty quid at the end of the week and nothing more. I used to look enviously at groups rehearsing around us, like I remember seeing The Move rehearsing in Birmingham, and I knew they would make it because they had so much drive. But our band didn't have any drive at all. It was held together by loyalty.

Elton with Tina Turner at the party following the New York première of The Who's *Tommy* movie in 1975.

I got so depressed playing 'Knock On Wood' every night. So I gave him *(Baldry)* notice.

Going Solo

Immediately after his final gig with Bluesology Reg Dwight became Elton John...
I'd had a terrible inferiority complex as Reg Dwight and the name change helped me to get out of it. Later I thought of changing it again but no-one could come up with anything better.

(Reg Dwight) was hopeless... it sounded like a library assistant. One of the guys in the group was Elton Dean, whose name I had always thought was real spiffy. I figured I could take part of his name but not all or he'd kick up. So I put it together with part of John Baldry's name and there it was... Elton John.

I couldn't get used to it *(being called Elton)*, but very few people call me Reg now - even Dick *(James)* has started calling me Elton, which is very strange.

I had to do something and I didn't want to join another band because quite honestly I wasn't that good an organist and I didn't look that good either. Really I wanted to be a singer but who would consider employing me in that capacity? Although I didn't really want to write I continued to toy with the idea because I thought that was the only way I'd get anywhere.

But it was the bravest thing I ever did to change from being a member of a backing group, not singing at all and playing organ rather badly, to going solo. It was a monumental decision, I didn't have anything to fall back on, and I knew that I wouldn't be able to join another group because I wasn't that good as an organist.

Bernie Taupin.

Elton auditioned for Liberty Records and through them met lyricist Bernie Taupin...
At my audition for Liberty Records I was asked to do five songs. But all I knew was 'He'll Have To Go' and 'I Love You Because'. They turned me down and I don't blame them.

I was impressed by Bernie's work. And I was keen to team up with him. Although I'd have been keen to team up with anyone. Dick James signed us, and he also signed me as a singer and not just as a songwriter. It was a tremendous break. I could leave Bluesology without financial worries.

It was ridiculous how many people were making demos up at Dick James studio, but one day he discovered what was going on and had a big purge, finding out just who was using his facilities. 'Who the

Elton and Bernie soon after 'Empty Sky' was recorded.

hell are Reg Dwight and Bernie Taupin?' he shouted, and he got Caleb *(Quaye)* to play some of the stuff we'd recorded. I don't think he was very impressed, but he agreed to sign us because Caleb, who was his blue-eyed boy, said he thought it was good. So we signed with Dick James for three years, or whatever, as songwriters and he guaranteed us ten quid a week each. That was less than I was getting in the group, but it was all I needed; so I gave my notice in.

Actually I did go for an interview with BEA *(British European Airways)* but my mother never discouraged me at all. I mean every time Taupin and I felt like giving up she'd say 'Right, piss off... go on, there's a job going up the greengrocer's, and we'd mumble something about that's not what we want to do.

The first thing we wrote together *(with Bernie Taupin)* was a thing called 'Scarecrow', then there was a song called 'One Time, Sometime Or Never' which Spencer Davis was going to record. When we started Bernie's lyrics would never be in verse form; there'd just be 115 lines and I'd say 'Where the fuck do I start?' But it didn't seem that difficult once I'd got used to it. In those days the songs were much more complex because the form in which Taupin wrote wasn't the verse/chorus style.

So many times we were told that Tom Jones or Lulu or Cilla Black was going to record one of our numbers and we used to go home thinking we'd finally made it. But nothing would materialise, because basically the songs were crap.

He *(Steve Brown, a song plugger at Dick James Music, one-time baritone sax player with Emile Ford and The Checkmates, who produced Elton's single 'Lady Samantha', and the first album 'Empty Sky')* told us our songs were not much good and that we should write the way we felt rather than with the charts in mind. It was very courageous of him.

Bernie and I were writing prolifically... total rubbish. But I was prolifically doing demos of the songs, and we made them into an album, produced by Caleb on a two-track machine. There were songs on it like 'Regimental Sergeant Zippo', and 'Watching The Planes Go By', but of all the songs we wrote in that era, only a couple have ever seen the light of day; there's one called 'The Tide Will Turn For Rebecca' - a Johnny Mathis-type thing that Edward Woodward recorded - and the other one was called 'I Can't Go On Living Without You' which Dick James put in for the Eurovision Song Contest. It got to the last six, the year that Lulu did the songs.

Elton and Bernie in 1992.

I made 'I've Been Loving You' as Elton John... not many people know that. Most people think that 'Lady Samantha' was the first. 'I've Been Loving You' was a sort of Engelbert Humperdinck type of thing.

I got approached by Jeff Beck, who said 'Listen, I want to join your band'. So I said 'All Right'. I was a bit wary at first. I said, 'A thousand watts of guitar, I can't stand it' because I really wanted the group to be just piano, bass and drums. Anyway, I said 'Well, come and do an audition'. He was fine. He played very quietly and very tastefully and then he said, 'Well, I'm sorry but I want to throw out your drummer', and I made it plain that he was going to meet with violent opposition from me. And then he wanted to employ me, he wanted me to come and do a tour of the States and pay me money to be in his band, 10 per cent of what he was going to earn, and the original idea was for him to join our band. So it was either going to join him, or come to LA, so we thought 'Sod Jeff Beck, we'll go to LA' and we did, and we were really glad that we stuck on that because that's where we got lucky in Los Angeles. I mean I've got no hard feelings with Jeff Beck at all. I mean we didn't have any harsh words, he just couldn't understand it.

The Records

Once albums are finished I can't bear to listen to them.

Empty Sky

I'll always remember that session *(their first for the eventual 'Empty Sky' album)*; we hired an electric piano which was so abysmally out of tune that I had to play round a lot of notes. After it was finished, I listened to it and thought it awful. I told Steve Brown that he ought to stick to plugging... I was really brought down. Steve played it to the people around the BBC, however, and they liked it and as a result it got a remarkable amount of airplay and went on to sell about twenty thousand.

Making the 'Empty Sky' album still holds the nicest memories for me, because it was the first I suppose. We used to walk back from the sessions at about four in the morning and stay at the Salvation Army headquarters in Oxford Street. Steve Brown's dad used to run the place, and he used to live above it. I used to sleep on the sofa. It's difficult to explain the amazing enthusiasm we felt as the album began to take shape, but I remember when we finished work on the title track... it just floored me. I thought it was the best thing I'd ever heard in my life.

How pompous some of my early songs were – just listen to 'Hymn 2000' on 'Empty Sky'.

Lady Samantha

I hated 'Lady Samantha' but Steve *(Brown)* liked it and it came out and got a reasonable amount of airplay.

Elton John

I got lucky, that's what happened. We released the 'Elton John' LP in England last May and it flopped. It sold about 4,000 copies or something ridiculous like that, and by quirk of fate we got a band together and we are beginning to do okay. (1971)

I had musical training a bit: I went to the Academy for five years every Saturday morning playing my Chopin Etudes and passed my grade examinations. When I listen to 'Elton John' I think, 'Christ, that's really sort of heavily classically influenced'.

I prefer orchestral stuff to piano music, and I prefer Mahler to Chopin. But when I listened to the 'Elton John' album again recently, it seemed so classically influenced. Everybody says that all my LPs sound the

Opposite:
Elton and Bernie accepting gold discs for the 'Elton John' LP.

same. But they can't say that about this one *('Honky Château')* because it's much happier and simpler.

A million groups did 'Pilot' and there were several versions of 'Sixty Years On' and 'Border Song', including a superb one by Aretha Franklin.

I know it sounds insane *(but)* I'd love to produce Dusty *(Springfield)*. When Dusty came up to me and said she thought 'Border Song' was a good record, I felt embarrassed. I didn't know what to say.

When we did the 'Elton John' album, we had 24 songs, two albums' worth of songs. And we fitted all the songs that could be lumped into an orchestral thing into one album. (1971)

Your Song

I think Bernie's lyrics are basically very uncommercial for the Top Twenty. 'Your Song' was an exception, it was a simple love song and people could identify with it.

If I had to choose from an EJ top five, I would never choose 'Your Song'. I've never understood it.

I don't think I'll ever be able to drop 'Your Song'. I sing it a bit like Billy Paul now because I really liked his version. I've sung 'Your Song' at every performance I've ever done, but that's the only one that's survived from the old set. (1973)

Tumbleweed Connection

'Ballad Of A Well Known Gun' was probably one of the first songs that Bernie and I ever wrote and I know people think that we really consciously put a theme of the Wild West into 'Tumbleweed' but it's really coincidental. Looking back now, it's really strange that it happened on that album like that. And it's funny because people get all these preconceived ideas about what happened. 'Son Of Your Father', for example, was recorded by Spooky Tooth a year and a half ago. It's just that Bernie's very interested in the Wild West. I get bored to tears by it all. If I see a Western on TV I switch off because I can't stand it. (1971)

UNI Records released 'Tumbleweed' in the States while 'Elton John' was still in the Top Ten there and it went straight into the charts at number 25 with a bullet. Within a couple of weeks we had two albums in the Top Five and when we got back home all the press suddenly wanted to know. Once we started getting all the publicity both those records zoomed up the charts in England too.

17.11.70

We have a live album *(out)* in three weeks which is really good. (1971)

I agree that the *(live)* album is not very good. During our second tour of the States, which was mostly co-headlining with people like Leon Russell, The Byrds, Poco and The Kinks, we were asked if we'd like to do a live broadcast over the air. We didn't know it at the time but afterwards we found out that Steve Brown had arranged for an 8-track recording to be made and when we listened to it we thought it was quite good. We did a quick mix at DJM and I wanted it to come out because Dee *(Murray)* and Nigel *(Olsson)* were featured very strongly. Looking back, it's not a wonderful recording but I think it's valid despite the fact that saleswise it was a disaster. Even 'Empty Sky' has outsold that one in Britain, and in America it only sold 325,000 copies, compared with the previous two which did over a million. But it did mean that I had four albums in the US Top Thirty at the same time which hadn't been done since The Beatles. (1972)

The live album '17-11-70', the 'Friends' soundtrack album, the 'Elton John' album and 'Tumbleweed Connection' - and it all looked like I was the overnight-sensation-in-a-year. I didn't want the albums out as they came. It was just circumstance.

Friends

We did the 'Friends' album in four weeks. Four weeks of very harrowing work. We did it at Olympic but for some reason got a terrible sound and had to do the whole lot again at Trident.

When we did the 'Friends' album we weren't known. When we were contracted to do it, we weren't really known anywhere and it's come out now. It's such a drag. (1971)

The album was done for experience and I would never ever do another soundtrack album. Actually the record was withdrawn, so if you've got a copy it's worth a small fortune.

Madman Across The Water

All I'm relieved about is that 'Madman' is the first album we've had that's a gold before release. And it's had good reviews almost everywhere. We really are album writers, Bernie and I. 'Empty Sky' bears up well, you know, I've got an eight-track of it and it was recorded back when the studio downstairs was a four-track.

Elton with DJ John Peel at the 1977 Reading Festival.

It's funny with 'Madman'... I can't listen to my vocals on that entire album. I hated it. Honestly, no bullshit, no Marc Bolan hype, it's my biggest catalogue seller... yet I can't listen to it. I can't listen to either 'Levon' or 'Tiny Dancer' because my vocals are so appalling but yet again that album was made under nightmare conditions. There were some unbelievable things going wrong through the making of it... *(Paul)* Buckmaster turning up for a session with no arrangements and 60 string players sitting there wondering what the hell was happening. And with all that going on... having just ten days to record the entire album. That's when I decided that the whole thing had to change.

When someone says the tracks on 'Madman' all sound the same I always disagree - the only reason I might agree is that sometimes the piano starts and then the bass comes in and then the drums and in that way it follows a format. That album was wrenched out of us because we had to produce an album for our record company, and we'd only had 'Madman' *(the song)* done as far as songs were concerned. Usually when we do an album we've got a stockpile of songs we can choose from. But because we were touring so much we didn't have a stockpile. (1972)

I was disappointed that it didn't make the charts *(it only reached number 41)* because I know the sale it did should have got it into the charts. I wouldn't have been worried if it didn't sell at all but it did sell. Not as well as we hoped, of course, but I really think it's because we stayed away and people do tend to forget.

Levon

I think I could have done better vocals on 'Levon' perhaps. It was in the wrong key, much too high.

It's about a guy who just gets bored doing the same thing. It's just somebody who gets bored with blowing up balloons and he just wants to get away from it but he can't because it's the family ritual.

Honky Château

He *(Bernie)* wrote 'Honky Château' while we were actually out in France in the studio. Well, studio... it's really a huge castle with a built-in studio. Hence the title of the album.

On 'Honky Tonk Château', Bernie would be upstairs writing away, then his wife Maxine would re-type it and bring it into the studio, and I'd put the melody to it there and then.

For a start there's no orchestra and there are rock'n'roll tracks which we've never done before on albums. I don't want to say it's the best thing I've ever done because that's what I said and felt about 'Madman' but people didn't agree. It's just that with this album no-one can turn around and say, 'Oh, it's Elton John with his bloody 100 piece orchestra again'. There's one number on the album called 'I Think I'm Going To Kill Myself' which I think is going to have tap dancing on it. A sort of vaudeville number. I guarantee the numbers on the album will get many covers because the songs are light pop. (1972)

Rocket Man

'Rocket Man' I never considered as a single until we got in there. When we first rehearsed the numbers for 'Honky Tonk Château' everyone said 'The Salvation' would be the single, but when we got in there it didn't work that way, so you can't tell. One song that won't be a single is a thing called 'All The Young Girls' which is about a lesbian.

Don't Shoot Me I'm Only The Piano Player

Once albums are finished I can't bear to listen to them. I can't listen to 'Don't Shoot Me' now, although I can play it on stage.

Daniel

It is one of the best songs we've ever written. I don't care if it's a hit or not.

I can't believe it but my manager doesn't want to advertise my new single. He's my manager, my publisher and my record company. And he doesn't like the new single 'Daniel'. He says the single isn't commercial and it's coming out at the wrong time. He says it will harm the sales of the album. But I want it out. We've reached a compromise where if it's a hit, he'll pay for the advertising, but not before.

Goodbye Yellow Brick Road

We tried to put down 'Saturday Night' *(at Dynamic Studios in Jamaica)* but it sounded terrible. We spent three days in the studio attempting to get a decent sound but in the end we decided to quit and go back to the Château. Then overnight all our hire cars were driven away and we started to panic. Next they impounded all our equipment and wouldn't let us out of the hotel because the studio was supposed to pay our hotel expenses and it became quite frightening and there was most definitely a very dodgy feeling in Kingston towards us. If that wasn't enough there was a strike at Dynamic so every time we drove in there were loads of pickets at the gate. I've never been so glad to leave a place in my life.

'Yellow Brick Road' never started out as a concept album.
We just did 22 tracks, and I couldn't remember how many we had done, there were so many. Then the ones we wanted on the album were put in running order and I didn't do the running order at all. It just came out like that. I can see what people mean about a concept. It's like 'Tumbleweed' which didn't have a theme either but seemed to develop one. To me 'Yellow Brick' is the ultimate pop album. If you wanted to tell kids about pop music, you could play them that album, because it's got so many influences on it. It's very weird. I never think about my records. I didn't realise for instance that it had such a tragic theme. Some disc jockey in Philadelphia came up to said 'Hey, your new album... Bernie is so bitter these days!' And I listened again, and it's true. It is a very depressive album, although I had never thought about it like that before. (1973)

I don't like double albums as a rule. Ninety per cent of them are padded with long jams, eight minute cuts and the like. But 'Yellow Brick Road' is like the ultimate Elton John album. It's got all my influences from the word go - it encompasses everything I ever wrote, everything I've ever sounded like.

Elton on stage with Davey Johnstone (on guitar), Nigel Olsson (drums) and Kiki Dee.

Candle In The Wind

I thought we were going to get groans from people when we did the Marilyn Monroe song. We wrote it about nine months ago, when she was vaguely in vogue, and now since then, everything has happened.

'Candle In The Wind' is a song about Marilyn Monroe and it's a real beautiful song. It's the only song I've ever written where I get goose bumps every time I play it.

Step Into Christmas

The Christmas single is a real loon about and something we'd like to do a lot more of. We've never written a song especially tailored to be a single. Up until now something's just been taken off the album and come out months later. This time we wrote it last Sunday morning, recorded it in the afternoon, and it'll be out this Friday.

I'm a sucker for Christmas singles and the fact that everyone else has Christmas singles coming out makes it more exciting – Slade have got one out.

Lucy In The Sky With Diamonds

We wanted to do some other people's songs on stage and Bernie suggested 'Lucy In The Sky'... and it went down a storm on gigs here *(in the UK)*. And he decided to see what it would sound like if we recorded it. We fancied having a different sort of single out anyway. We wanted to see how it would go with another John Lennon song on the back. John Winston liked it anyway, and I was quite pleased with the way it came out.

People criticised me for recording Beatle material. To me, a great song will always stand the test of time.

Caribou

I'm trying to get things simpler all the time, to get away from arrangements and make things looser. Not as loose as the Stones or Faces – more like Joni Mitchell.

I've been nominated for the Grammy Award's Best Vocal Performance for 'Don't Let The Sun Go Down On Me'. After I did the vocal on that one I went to Gus *(Dudgeon, Elton's producer)* and I said, 'If you put this on the album I'll sodding well shoot you'. I thought it was the worst vocal of all time, and I said, 'I hate the song. I hate my vocals'.

When I record I like to have things done straight away. Making 'Caribou' was a very trying experience. Really, the whole album was

put together by Gus because we all pissed off to Australia and Japan.
He got The Beach Boys and Tower of Power together and did
it on his own.

It was recorded under the most excruciating of circumstances.
We had eight days to do fourteen numbers. We did the backing tracks
in two and a half days. It drove us crazy because there was a huge
Japanese tour, then Australia and New Zealand, that could not be
put off. And it was the first time we had recorded in America, and
we just couldn't get adjusted to the monitoring system which was
very flat. I never thought we'd get an album out of it.
'Caribou' wasn't meant, it was a miracle it came out.

I can understand why 'Caribou' was criticised, although I didn't
think it was a bad album. I knew it wouldn't get accepted as well as
'Yellow Brick Road' because it was just a light album. 'Yellow Brick
Road' was impossible to follow. I knew that. I thought there was
no way we would follow it with a titanic effort again. (1974)

I thought 'Caribou' would get slagged off because it seemed
the time for something of mine to get slagged. I think the British press
might have decided it's time to knock me again, so I'm just sitting back
and taking it. I knew I would get some bad reviews but it's just
a period. (1974)

Greatest Hits

It was an obvious time to put a 'Greatest Hits' out, because it
would have meant a year without any product by the time the next
album comes out. I didn't think it would do so well (it topped both
the US and UK charts). It's the fastest ever MCA record in America.
The figures are just stupid. It's quite a good album because most of it,
apart from 'Border Song' which I wanted to stick on although it wasn't
a sales hit, was recorded when people really started taking notice.
They wanted to put a hits album out last year – you know what
record companies are like when they've got product to merchandise –
but we said no, because there was no point in it last year. It would
have been filled with things that weren't hits. This year I thought it
would be good. (1974)

Captain Fantastic And The Brown Dirt Cowboy

Bernie has the idea of writing about how we met. I have a feeling that
it won't be commercial but I never know what is and what isn't.

It was entirely about us *(me and Taupin)*. The whole album was
written from my end on the *SS France* going from Southampton to
New York. I tried to get the music room but an opera singer had it

Bernie - The Brown Dirt Cowboy.

booked the whole time except for when she scoffed her lunch for two hours. So every two hours at lunch time I used to go in there and nip out to the piano and I wrote the whole of the 'Captain Fantastic' album.

By the time 'Captain Fantastic' comes out, it'll have been a year between new albums, excluding the 'Greatest Hits' one, and I'm glad about that. I think it was the right time to do the 'Greatest Hits' one, there's enough material. But with the pressure off to do a set number of albums, who knows? We may do four albums a year, maybe one.

It's a story type album about how Bernie and I got together, so if ever anybody asks that question again, it's all there. There's personal things and business things about how we started on £10 a week. It's not a concept album, but I'm so pleased with the songs. I think it wipes the floor with 'Yellow Brick Road' and this is the first album we've ever spent five weeks on. Gus (Dudgeon) mixed three or four different versions of each track and I chose which one I thought was best, or nearest the mark.

The album is called 'Captain Fantastic And The Brown Dirt Cowboy'. I'm Captain Fantastic and Bernie's the Brown Dirt Cowboy. It's based on our experiences together up until the time we made 'Empty Sky' - how we met, the various problems, trying to get money out of people.

'We All Fall In Love' is probably about Bernie and I. As far as I'm concerned the song is about Bernie and I realising we had a future together. Not a sexual future but a brother relationship, which we still have. We are still like close brothers. It's about the realisation that we could make it. Really, it says it all in that song.

Elton and Bernie mining precious metal.

'Curtains' is saying, really we did write crap, we were naïve, but who the fuck wasn't? When you listen to everybody's records when they first start off everybody has their ideas which they tend to overdo.

The reviews did make me feel that maybe we'd been a bit self-indulgent. But for me it's a completely honest album. I've laid myself on the line. It's the truth and I don't see why people should criticise me for being autobiographical. For me it will always be my favourite album. But that's from a purely selfish point of view. Whether it will stand the test of time, who knows? (1975)

'Captain Fantastic' is more than autobiography, it's a study of two people's ambivalent love–hate relationship with success. There's a surprising amount of anger in the lyrics. It's quite a bitter album because everybody has to pay their dues. I can't think of anyone who hasn't been through unhappy times getting screwed while trying to be successful. But it's also a happy album for me. I laugh a lot remembering those unhappy times. (1975)

'Captain Fantastic' became the first album ever to go straight to number one in the US Billboard charts in the week of release…
It was a pinnacle for me. That's as big as I got. It was a time when you couldn't switch a radio on in America without hearing one of my songs and people do get cheesed off. I was cheesed off with hearing myself as well and that's why I started, instead of just doing albums, to try and do the occasional odd single.

Pinball Wizard

You've not heard the great Rod Stewart story? Ah lovely, it's great. Originally, when the 'Tommy' film was discussed a long long time ago, at the time when that bloody album came out, which I hated, Rod approached me one day and said, 'They're going to do a film of 'Tommy', and I said, 'Oh no, not a film now. Bloody hell, what are they going to do next? It will be a cartoon series soon'. Rod told me they wanted him as the Pinball Wizard and I said, 'I should knock it on the head if I was you'. So a year went by and they were trying to get the world and his mother to do it. I was offered loads of parts in it and I always said no. Then I found out Ken Russell was doing it, and I spoke to Pete *(Townshend)* about it, and became quite enthusiastic about the idea. To cut a long story short, I ended up doing the Pinball Wizard and, of course, Stewart when he found out couldn't believe it. 'You bastard…' Quite an amusing story. (1974)

I have to wear these four and a half foot shoes, which Russell, of course, made me walk in. The Wizard doesn't look like a Mod, no, not at all. I've got a Lurex hat with a big big bobble Christmas decoration on top.

Blue Moves

The trouble with making an album is that I always feel I've got to try and please everybody - an impossible task! I tried not to do that with 'Blue Moves', and as a result, it worked out quite well.

Simplicity is something I'm very keen to get back to. I think my work's been getting a little bit too fussy lately.

A Single Man

'Single Man' was an album that wasn't meant to be an album. I went into the studio and did a record of 'Ego' which was a two-year-old song Bernie and I had written. And because I hadn't written for so long I got writer's diarrhoea as I call it and suddenly I began to write melodies first. Gary *(Osborne)* was around and I had a few ideas for a certain line to the songs, and certain titles, and we had great fun doing it.

Song For Guy

While I was writing the music I couldn't stop thinking about death. It was as though someone else was guiding my hand.

I wrote the song one Sunday when I was feeling very depressed.

Victims Of Love

I know everyone thinks that's what they like but I want to try different things, too. I know I am going to get knocked for the album. It all started when an old friend Pete Bellotte, who has been working on Donna Summers' album for a few years, asked if I'd like to do a disco album with him.

It didn't do my career a lot of good but I don't regret doing it whatsoever. I can understand why it wasn't successful. I enjoyed it, it was self-indulgent, but in the next few years people will have to expect more self-indulgent things from me to appear.

Too Low For Zero

'Too Low For Zero' is very important for me. I've lived with it for so long and wouldn't change anything on it.

There's no getting away from it there is a certain magic whenever we work together. *('Too Low For Zero', in 1983, was Elton's first full collaboration with Bernie Taupin since 1976.)*

Reg Strikes Back

My last album 'Reg Strikes Back' did very well in England.
It's just gone cardboard.

Sleeping With The Past

The first thing I've done for years when I was feeling good, without
any personal problems or lawsuits hanging over my head. I think that's
why it's such an up album. It's a very R&B sort of thing. It isn't so
diverse as some of my earlier albums, it has the same feel throughout,
but Bernie and I both think it's my best work in years.

The One

I think we're both very happy with 'The One' album, not so
with some albums. I've sometimes been happy, he's been miserable,
I've been miserable, he's been happy or we've both been miserable,
but on this album we've both clicked.

The Last Song

It made me cry when I wrote it and I broke down when I was doing
the demo and I just cried and cried. Freddie had just died a few weeks
before, and so many of my friends have died, and it's... just a very
touching thing.

Rocket Records

We got very drunk one night, and David Johnstone, my guitarist,
told me he wanted to make an album but couldn't find anyone to help
him do it. The idea grew, and now I have spent several thousand
pounds setting the whole thing up. First single on the new label -
Rocket Records - is called 'If It Was So Simple', and is by a group

called Longdancer. I can't record on the label yet for contractual
reasons, but I might decide to do so at some future date.

Kiki *(Dee)* was the first person we signed to our own Rocket label,
and it just seemed natural that we should try and do something for her.
I was very proud to write for her - she really is an incredible singer.

I want it *(speaking of his new company and label Rocket)* to be
available for unknown people to get decent treatment, and I want to
be involved. I don't want it to become a huge complex. Where are
they all now? Where are the new Beatles or Stones who are going to
come along and shake us all out of our complacency? It's all become
so solemn and so static. I can see Lennon still a teenage idol at 40.

We were offered Queen and Cockney Rebel but we turned them
down simply because we couldn't afford them. We were even offered
10cc - but again they want far too much money up front to sign with
the label. What a lot of groups fail to realise is that the days have gone
now when you went with a record company and got well and truly
screwed. Sure some people are still being screwed but mainly because
of old contracts. The heaviest thing we ever paid out was Casablanca
but that was my fault because I suggested that we sign them to Rocket.
And it's just very unfortunate that they didn't work out.

Our ideas still haven't changed *(at Rocket after a year or so of operation)*,
it's just the first year was a nightmare, really, because we made so many
mistakes. We signed a few acts that we shouldn't have signed and we
thought it was going to be easy, and it's so difficult.

Elton with Kiki Dee following the première of
Blood Brothers.

It's very hard running a record company. I didn't realise it was going
to be so hard. But I think the fault was just the lack of communication
between the five directors - me, Bernie, Gus Dudgeon, Steve Brown
and John Reid... by the end of it all we had hundreds of meetings,
I was so cheesed off I just had to go away on my own, which is
something I've never done before. I just pissed off to Arizona, I just
couldn't take it.

Bootlegs

It's funny to think people want to hear your stuff so desperately
they'll buy a bootleg album, or that people will go to the trouble of
manufacturing a bootleg album because they know the demand is
there. We've got two going for us in the States at the moment.
One is called 'Very Live' which is the radio thing. The other thing
is called 'Rubba Dubba' and has me and Leon Russell together at
Berkeley. Our publisher in the States is sending a copy for us to
listen to. He says it's been pressed on yellow see-through vinyl or
something totally ridiculous.

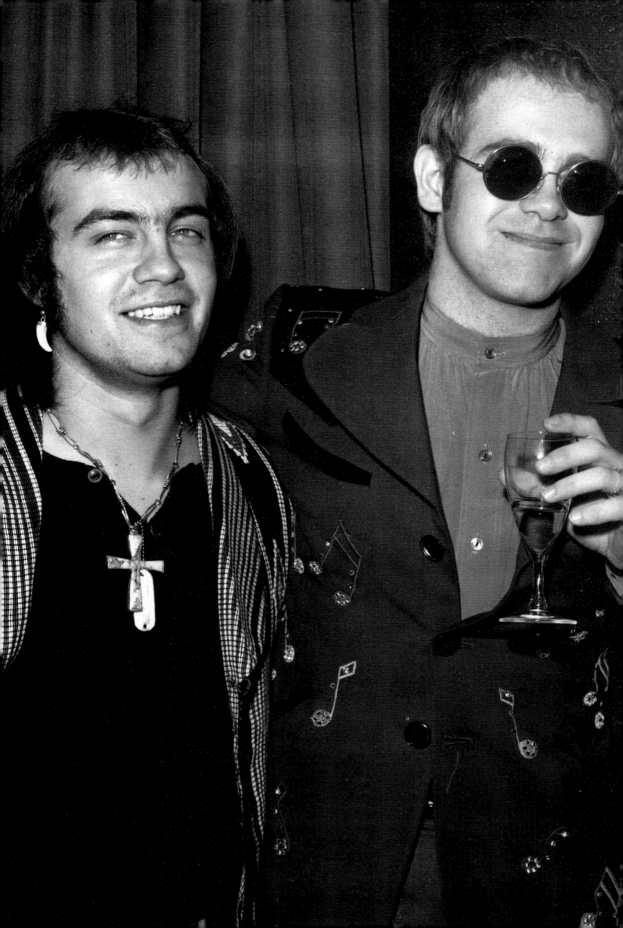

Songwriting

With Bernie Taupin...
I really don't know what's going on in Bernie's mind. I ask him
if a certain song is about a certain person or something like that,
but I don't get any sense out of him.

Songwriting isn't as lucrative as playing or anything else. I mean
Bernie's earned probably less money out of it by far than any of the
band or anybody.

I was just lucky to find somebody who could write lyrics, because
I could never have got them together. We've been through so many
funny things together, so many hard times and disappointments, that
we're sort of like brothers, really. All his lyrics are just talking fantasies,
so all I'm doing, in fact, is singing Bernie's fantasies. I know that and
I enjoy it. I didn't meet him until I'd written the music to about
ten of his lyrics.

I can just have instant lyrics from Bernie and it doesn't take me more
than 15 minutes if I'm in the mood to write the music. (1973)

I didn't find it difficult writing for a girl *(Kiki Dee)* but I think
Bernie had a bit of trouble with the lyrics. He found it hard to see
things from a female point of view, as you can imagine. We're not
really the public's idea of a songwriting team. You know two guys
sweating over a hot piano, shirtsleeves rolled up, shades on. We're
very unprofessional. I think too many people are doing their own
songs and not enough people are covering other people's songs – you
can do someone else's song and you can do it well and you don't have
to stick to the same bloody arrangements and very few people with the
exception of Aretha Franklin, Al Kooper and Billy Paul have done
anything different with them all and I think you can do some amazing
things. Joe Cocker did with 'A Little Help From My Friends' and
there's a lot of singers that could do. I think the trouble with most
people today is that they stick to one sort of music and there's so
much good music going around. I just wish artists would try and
listen to other sides of music because I think it does you good.

He only writes about personal things which is great. Because I
know him inside out and when I get the lyrics I know exactly what
he's talking about.

He hates me to say 'write a song with someone's name in it'.

Too many groups write their own material and a lot of it is
substandard; not everyone can be a songwriter. They should learn to

ki Dee with her cardboard cut-out of Elton.

recognise what is good material and what isn't, there's not enough taste and discrimination. That's why Bernie and I only produce 15 or 16 songs a year, that's all that reaches the standard we set. I mean think about the great songwriters today, someone like Paul Simon, how many does he produce? Not very many, it would surprise you if you counted them.

Bernie always writes the lyrics first, and then I take a look at them and later I'll sit down at the piano and put them to music. I always start at the top and work through to the bottom. No song ever takes me more than half an hour, and then I forget about it until we come to record it.

I didn't really want to be labelled as a songwriter, because people would immediately put us in the same bag as Tony Macauley and Bacharach and David. That's not to put them down in any way, it's just not what I want.

In 1978 Elton and Bernie ceased working together, and Gary Osborne became Elton's temporary lyricist...
I intended to work again with Gary Osborne and, depending upon his reaction to this album, to collaborate again with Taupin, but he might be dreadfully upset because there's not one track of his on the new album. He'll probably feel extremely hurt but it'll give him a much-needed kick up the arse.

I think the trouble with most people today is that they stick to one sort of music and there's so much good music going around. I just wish artists would try and listen to other sides of music because I think it does you good. I think I've never known how I felt – that's why I haven't been able to write lyrics.

I'm getting better, but I feel like a stuttering baby trying to learn how to speak. *(Speaking of his own efforts to write words.)*

Somehow I can never get what I'm thinking out through a pen and on to paper – it's very frustrating. I'd like to write more instrumental things, too. I always enjoy those. Still, there's plenty of time for all that.

Songwriters who are just starting out, all they can do for the first two or three years is hope. All the money you get in advance doesn't compensate for one person saying keep it going, 'cos there's something there. Very few people said that to us. Only about two or three.

I'm beginning to get a bit fed up with singer-songwriter records. They drive me mad. I was labelled a singer-songwriter and did four

ton and Bernie with DJM boss Dick James.

albums in that syndrome. People take us seriously. I'd like us to be
a band. On the first albums we used a lot of session men, but we could
never do it that way now, planning it down to the last flute.

I listen to practically every new album that comes out.
Not because I'm trying to pinch ideas but because I'm interested in
finding out what's happening. If you take the standard of our albums
compared to other people, the standard is so much higher. I read
a great review of an album in a music paper and I immediately rush
out and buy it. And some of those albums wouldn't even grace making
into an ashtray. It just seems that people are drastically searching for
something red hot and they're not really finding it, and they're
turning to crap and saying that's good. (1974)

I don't know what a hit single is. I can pick other people's
hit singles. I've never intentionally attempted to write a hit single.
During my entire career *(up to 1975)*, the only things I've ever stuck
out for have been 'Daniel' and 'Don't Let The Sun Go Down On
Me'. I just liked the song *('Daniel')* and it meant a lot to me.

I don't have any conscious influences, but I listen to a lot of music
and there are so many people I admire and who must have had an
effect on me... The Band, Van Morrison, Neil Young... people like
Zappa and Jagger, who don't give a shit. Zappa - well, I don't believe
he exists, and Jagger is the most underrated vocalist.

We've learned to let everything drop out of the charts before putting
out something else.

I like good pop records. I just do it instantaneously. I never get
a thought that might be an idea for a song because I just forget it.
When I write a song it usually comes literally in half an hour.
If it's not there in half an hour I give up, and say 'Well, I'll
try it again'.

Songs are very easy to write. I can't believe some people take a
year and a half and come out with a really substandard album of things
you've heard before.

I don't know how to evaluate my music. Does that sort of thing
appeal to Led Zeppelin fans? It's very strange. I don't think I'm a great
player by any means. (1973)

I'd hate to have to record in a very big one *(studio)*... they're
like being in hospital, terribly clinical, with no atmosphere at all.
For me a studio has to be cosy and a bit moody, and Trident's like
that. Another advantage is that there the drums are contained in a
little booth of their own, completely shut off from everything, so
there's almost perfect separation and no leakage of sound to speak of.
They can also get a marvellous string sound there, but it's a bit of
a mystery why. Most studios that are good for strings have high
ceilings, but Trident has a low one and it's still great. We use about
21 strings usually. Probably 'Empty Sky' was the first time I had sung
seriously, but I still like it in a funny way. Yeah, it sounds a lot
more British than I do now, but then I'm a spade freak so I try to
sound like a spade in a lot of ways. Spades try to sound like whites too.
It's not just a one-way thing. The Temptations and all that, they can't
wait to break into the cabaret bit, 'My Way', and things.

I am obsessed with work, producing and creating good records.
I am in the rock and roll business. That means I want to play as much
rock and roll as I possibly can.

Molly, the tea lady at the football club... she puts me in my place,
and tells me when she thinks my records are not as good as they
should be.

I spend quite a lot of money getting all the singles from America
and I study the charts in both American and British papers so that
I always have the latest records on my jukebox. Actually it works out
quite expensive, because besides the records on the jukebox, I like to
have another copy of it for my collection, and a cassette of the same
record for my machine in the house and the stereo in my car. So that's
four copies of each record. 'Ziggy Stardust' is my favourite album of
the year. And I like very much the record he *(David Bowie)* produced
for Mott the Hoople, 'All The Young Dudes'. I keep playing it on my
jukebox. I just hope he doesn't go too far or freaky.

I do listen to most things that are happening on the music scene
but I confess I find rap is not my bag.

Performing

Even if I had only one finger left, I'd play for you.

I didn't want to be a performer. I would sooner have stayed at home writing songs. But I'm having the time of my life. (1970)

I don't want to sit down and do slow things all night. I'd go to sleep. I've been a rock'n'roll freak for a long time but people seem to think that I have to do rock'n'roll just to prove that I'm a hip young man. Well... I was brought up on rock'n'roll. I've always been into rock'n' roll. That's my favourite sort of music. The Rolling Stones are my idols and that's it. (1971)

Rock'n'roll music is the most important music to me. So I'm not going to sit there and sing all these boring songs. Everybody wants me to be like Randy Newman which is a drag because Randy Newman is fantastic. (1971)

After the 'Elton John' album everyone thought I was going to come out on stage and be very sensitive like Peter Skellern.

The kids wanted to hear the noise. They just like to have their ear drums splattered.

I'd really like to do a couple of gigs a week, because that's how you sell yourself to people. *Top Of The Pops* doesn't really give anybody an idea of what you can do... in fact it gives them a totally wrong impression.

We were only in the States for about three weeks, but the whole experience changed our lives. We were living in a cage of hype all the time, but nevertheless we did get to meet some nice people. It seemed we spent most of our time going round offices shaking hands with people.

The show *(the 1972 Royal Variety Performance)* was the most horrific experience of my life. I'm not a violent person but I came close to socking Sir Bernard Delfont right on the nose. Backstage pressures, lack of sound amplification, too many acts packed into four hours... it was carnage. Princess Margaret has told me she thinks it's four hours of boredom. More artists turn the Royal Show down. The only reason the Royal Family suffer it is because the money goes to a charitable cause.

I mean now all you can see is people coming in see-through dresses, and me sitting at the piano singing 'Your Song' with a beautiful back-

Nigel Olsson, Dee Murray, Elton and Davey Johnstone.

ground. It's rubbish! We're creating the new show-biz which I've always wanted to try and avoid; you know, becoming another sort of Sammy Davis Junior or something like that. *(Speaking about playing music on television.)*

The trip was made much easier this time because we hired a private jet, the Starship 1, which meant we could base ourselves in one hotel and then fly out to each individual gig. Led Zeppelin used it on their last tour as well. It's fantastic inside with bathrooms and showers, a living room, bedroom, huge bar, two video television sets and a Hammond organ. The only trouble is that as I don't take a large entourage the bloody thing looked half empty most of the time. The eight of us felt as if we were playing hide and seek.

The policemen can be a bit of trouble there *(America)*, I've physically shoved them off the stage before - taking my life in my own hands - because they've been standing up right in front of the stage. At one open air concert I said come down to the front, and Nigel was virtually playing with people in the bass drum! I was told if you don't get rid of them they'll be trouble, so I had to ask everyone to move back - do my Winston Churchill bit! - but I think they take more notice of English artists when they say that. I'm not sure that they'd take it from someone like Sly.

The kids are there and they've paid to see you. You go on and that's your audience. They're loyal. They'll buy your records. They don't get the freebies from the record companies. They're the ones who put you where you are and you're really geared up to give them a good show. That's when I really enjoy myself. (1972)

It's very important to pace an act. We could go on stage and
do twenty new numbers but people don't want to hear that. Critics
sometimes do, but the audiences don't.

I'm not a serious performer anyway – just somebody who is
having a go at the piano. I do the best I can. I don't consider myself as
a dedicated performer – I can't see myself performing till I drop dead.
(1972)

The band is trying to talk me into playing organ, but I hate it.
I hated playing organ and I'm terrible. I only had a Vox Continental
(with Bluesology) and I wouldn't really play that. It's because I've got a
fat arse. It's a completely different kettle of fish playing an organ to a
piano. You've really got to study organ because a Hammond is bloody
hard to play. Keith Emerson knows it inside out, knows all the stops
and drawbars. I'm too lazy. I just can't be bothered.

I'd like to go out there in front of a Grateful Dead audience but
that sort of audience have got a prejudice built up against you before
you start. I'm sure I could go out on stage and outrock anybody in
the world because when I've been second on the bill to anyone I've
thought 'Right you bastards'... I don't really mean it but you have
to go with that sort of attitude.

The stage, in reality, is the closest you can ever get to most of
the fans. They may say hello backstage or in a hotel or something.
But even that is not as close as seeing a show and being affected by
the music. That's why I get upset if I play badly. Not only for me,
but because I know I've disappointed the audience. .

It took me over a year to find out how to amplify the piano.
I use nine ordinary microphones and it took the roadie a year and
a half working on it. I've tried the most incredibly complicated contact
mixes. You pin them on separately, and they've made the piano sound
like an electric piano. It's very hard to get a natural sound.

Elton with Kiss.

Playing television is difficult. The only thing I'd be interested in doing is something like that *(six groups or artists in the studio, and just have them play together, and televised live)* where everything is chaotic and live and exciting. Greedy promoters. I don't know anything about it. Greedy artist is more like it. I just want to go out there and play.

We're doing one new number on stage – I don't want to make this mistake of going on stage and playing five new numbers because by the time you do record them you're probably sick of them, so we're just going to do an up-tempo thing called 'Love Lies Bleeding'.

While I'm on stage I'm happy because I'm close to the fans and when things are going well it's just one big family. That's a great feeling.

Why do you think I kick away at the piano at a certain point in my act? It's because that was the music that I came up with. I find it fun.

Top: Kenny Passarelli (bass), Davey Johnstone (guitar), Caleb Quaye (guitar) and Elton.

Bottom: Nigel Olsson, Legs Larry Smith, Elton, Davey Johnstone and Dee Murray.

I couldn't compete with the Bowies or Jaggers. I haven't got the figure for it. I'd look like Donald Dumpling from Dover, so I try and make people grin a bit. It's probably reacted against me a bit, but that's exactly the effect I wanted.

I think we play better in America. I think we play twice as well. But I don't know why. I can't put my finger on it. It's this feeling you get when you're over there. Just the whole atmosphere. Bigger somehow, better. It all moves fast, it's big time. England is a bit lazy, isn't it?

I can't understand those people who say they don't like doing concerts. The stage, in reality, is the closest you can ever get to most of the fans. That's why I get very upset if I play badly. Not only for me, but because I know I've disappointed the audiences.

I think this is my final line-up. I don't think I'll go through changing bands again. Five years with one band was great. I think this band will be a better band eventually because there's a lot more scope musically. (1975)

In 1976 Elton decided to cut back on his hectic touring schedule…
I feel like stopping for a time. I've done it for six years and I'm fed up

John Reid.

with it. I'm not so much fed up with playing but I'm fed up with
having no base and constantly roaming around. I just want to spend
time doing other things that I want to do. It's a shame in a way
because the band is just beginning to feel its way on stage. I just have
to give it up for a while. I say that now but I could change my mind.
I'm not retiring. I just want to lay off for a bit. (1976)

It came to the point where I sang 'Yellow Brick Road' and
I thought, 'I don't have to sing this any more' and it made me quite
happy inside. I'm definitely not retiring but I want to put my energies
elsewhere for a while. I always do things by instinct and I just know
it's time to cool it. I mean, who wants to be a 45-year-old entertainer
in Las Vegas like Elvis. (1976)

Quite suddenly I got fed up seeing people's faces squashed
against fences. I thought 'Well, this might be great for me but is it so
great for them?' It wasn't normal. I had to stop. Rethink. (1976)

Having no permanent base, continually living in hotel rooms
was affecting me. It got to a point where I remembered things that
had happened to me before all the success better than I remembered
the last three or four years. I finally had to say 'stop!'

I get immense pleasure from what I'm doing. I think it's very
rewarding. But I certainly ain't appearing at Batley Variety Club or
playing the Talk Of The Town when I'm 40, because there's more
to life than that. (1977)

I hadn't decided to say it before I went on stage, so of course
I didn't tell him. I think he had about five heart attacks all at once.
(His retirement announcement and the effect on manager John Reid.)

People will lose the memory of that outrageous guy looning
around on stage at the piano. I'll become something else, it'll be
different. I'll do it. I've always known I'd be a success.

I was wrong. I didn't know how much I would miss it.
(After his comeback in 1979.)

But I don't think I'd make a very good full-time actor, not a
real one! I couldn't face going out on stage, night after night, saying
and doing the same things. I hate to admit it but I think I might get
bored. That's what's so good about rock shows - you can do your
own thing - within reason!

It's the greatest thing in the world to stand on a stage and see
people in the front rows smiling and know they came to see you.

What this business boils down to is playing songs and getting an audience with you. As long as I can do that things won't be so bad. I've never been able to play the guitar, though I'd like to. I just can't seem to master it. I'm not very good on the technicalities either. I'm hopeless when it comes to electronics. I couldn't even put a plug on the toaster.

I know my voice has improved 200 per cent because I have to sing in tune. I have to remember the words and I have to play the right chords. I never was nervous in the past with the band, but now I get physically sick with nerves every night.

I'm approaching middle-age and I don't want to go on touring when I'm 37 or 38.

I don't think I'm blameless, but I do consciously try to entertain people. I never wanted to. I just wanted to write songs. But now I'm on stage, I'm going to put a show on.

I know people say, 'Bloody hell, not him again!' but I'm totally in love with it (Performing).

I get so upset if I play badly. Not only for me, but because I know I've disappointed the audience. There's nothing worse than knowing everybody went home thinking 'oh boy, that sure was a drag'. That's what you struggle against every night. I think I go through periods when I think 'this isn't worth it' and I don't want to see anybody and I don't want to do anything. Everybody does, I guess.

I look back now and think, how the hell did I do that? I mean, I've really got it easy now. But it was a good grounding. That's where you learn. When you look back on it, you're glad you did it. I've paid my dues, and I never want to do it again.

I had to take a rest, a three-year vacation from what I was doing. I was tired out, I was burnt out, I had no creative juice left. I'd put out a lot of product – probably too much – I'd done too many tours. *(Speaking of the period post-'Sleeping With The Past'.)*

In 1979 Elton became one of the first Western rock performers to tour the USSR...
I wanted the challenge of playing somewhere without a predictable audience. When we were on stage in Leningrad for the first time, we didn't know how it would go. But it was just incredible.

The 'Nikita' video.

You must not put your feet on the keys of the Steinway grand piano, kick the piano stool, you must not sing The Beatles' song 'Back In The USSR' *(so Elton was told before he began the tour; he co-operated on the first two but not the third).*

The Russians wouldn't let us fly between Moscow and Leningrad. We had to go by train. We presume there was something they didn't want us to see.

I'm knocked out, this has to be my biggest achievement as an artist. These people don't have my records. They don't know my songs, and yet they reacted like that. I'm at a loss for words.

It was just amazing, incredible. Even if you don't know a word of the language, music speaks for you.

Psyche

I'm just a little fish waiting to be eaten... just an ordinary kind of boy.

I am self-destructive. I get terribly, stubbornly depressed. It's my desperate craving for affection coming out. I'll get in a mood and I'll sit at home for two days in bed, getting more and more depressed, wondering if it's all worth it, and all those silly thoughts. But I have friends who are very good to me. My manager *(John Reid)* can't help me when I'm depressed because he's my manager and I fight him. But Muff Winwood or Tony King will ring up and say, 'Well, run out of Pledge have we?' You know, I hoover and dust. Things like that are really good for my mind. I used to love ironing. It soothed me out. I'm one of those people who go around emptying ashtrays, washing them and putting them back. And so, as soon as I'm in a bad mood, one of my friends has only got to ring up and send me up a bit and I'll come out of it. (1975)

I can be very happy and then, all of a sudden, I'm on a come down. Depressions are very strange. They can come on in the most unlikely places and for no apparent reason. Perhaps I'm not so self-destructive as some artists, but I'm definitely self-destructive. Most artists are. I consider myself slightly insane in a funny way. I think I must be nuts somewhere along the line - just for wanting to keep going. (1975)

I had such a terrible inferiority complex and was so shy. I was confused and had no confidence in myself. My confidence grew with the success. I lived my teenage years in my twenties. (1984)

You can't get to 41 or 42 and carry it off gracefully. Some things have just got to come to an end.

I tried to be really nice to everyone but I ended up getting kicked in the teeth for it. Everything gets so out of hand in Britain. I just like getting credit for what we've done and nobody seems to be doing it.

I had no sex education at home. I didn't have sex at all until I was twenty-one, it was ridiculous. That's the sort of life I had. I was just a paranoiac, little, fat person, who was always being told to do something.

When I get fed up I dash around polishing and dusting everything in sight.

I often wish that when I sit down to do an interview that people would say 'Well, listen, you're a no-talented idiot, and you're very lucky, and why? And I think you're a bore.' And I really wish somebody would say that to me, but everybody's so nice! I remember an interview with a college kid in New York, and he worked for just an ordinary college paper, and I said, 'Yeah, I'll do the interview' and he came in and said 'I really don't like this. I think it's crappy rubbish,' and it completely slayed me. I said 'What do you mean?' I got really annoyed and we got down to it and we fought like cat and dog through the whole interview, and I really enjoyed it, and we were great friends afterwards. I just think people should say what they think sometimes. If they want to say that it's awful I don't really mind.

There have been so many inaccuracies about me. They say I spend thousands on a meal when in fact a record company was paying. I'm meant to be in places all over the world when in fact I'm playing a charity football match in Britain, the list is endless.

It was near enough a nervous breakdown. I was, in fact, mentally unstable. I couldn't go out of the house without breaking down in tears. That's the reason. I couldn't go to see football matches.

Couldn't go anywhere. I tried being positive. Told myself to stop feeling so sorry for myself. Come on, pull yourself together. It didn't work. So I went into hiding. Just didn't see the point of making a spectacle of myself in public. And that failure upset me. (1988)

I'd love to be able to switch to wherever I wanted to, especially in the future. I'd like to know if it's going to be as horrific as I think it will.

If I'm at a party and someone says 'How about singing us something from your new album?' I get the same feeling *(embarrassment)*. In any case I go to a party to enjoy myself. (1972)

I'm not a very patient person. I always lose and I hate losing. I might as well admit it.

You do get hurt *(by critics)*, but only for about five minutes. It's no good moping about it. You have to take the good with the bad, otherwise you wouldn't be in this business. I think I've had more than my fair share of criticism but that's all right with me. I think now I've got over the bulk of the criticism. What you've got to realise is that no two people are alike and nobody likes exactly the same as you.

I have a great reputation for opening my mouth, and then two years later doing completely the opposite.

I'm more or less thinking I'll have to start from the word go again. It's a healthy attitude for me because it is very easy to get complacent. Thinking this way kicks me up the rear. *(When he reached 30.)*

I'm so ambitious it's incredible. And criticism has always driven me on. I'm the kind of person who lets himself get kicked in the teeth and the more that happens, the more I thrive on it. I don't know if that's the masochist in me or what it is that makes me like having hell beaten out of me. I always strive to do something that will get a reaction –even if it's to make people angry.

I suppose I'm a bit like Alice Cooper in that way – any chance I get to meet someone I really admire I take. I think it's always good to have idols, people you respect, and I've got more sporting heroes than anything else. I think you need to be a special kind of person to be a top sportsman. Anyone can be a rock star. Wanna make a record? There's a lot more dedication in being a tennis champion than being a rock musician – like I'm sure The Rolling Stones don't get up every morning and have a rehearsal. Rock'n'roll is far more loose, far more fun, but I can't imagine a bigger thrill than scoring a goal in the World Cup or something.

The thing about rock'n'roll is that I don't have to take it seriously.

That's one thing I really get paranoid about – meeting people who make records nowadays. I feel so terribly old. I feel like Frank Sinatra going up to Boy George. I don't know what to say to them. (1984)

I love sitting in kitchens, they're always so cosy. When I was a kid we always sat around in the kitchen. The lounge was a special place for special occasions as you couldn't just come thundering in from football and scatter mud all over it. And there was never such a thing as a dining room! That just didn't exist. I always feel much more relaxed in the kitchen because you're right in the middle of everything.

I still live a complicated lifestyle, but I was all outside and no inside before. What you saw was what you got, but inside was something totally different. Now my insides are happy, and I feel refreshed and ready to start again.

I love blasting out music as I drive around, it's one of life's great joys.

I've always retained my urge to compete, though at times I have recorded too many albums – music has always been my life.

Elton on stage at Watford Football Club.

It's really funny because when I was struggling to make it and starving and being swindled I never ever got depressed. But now I'm always swearing I'm going to give up this business to go to Barbados and open a shop or something.

I was being very arrogant on stage and loving every minute of it. But coming off stage I didn't have the confidence to cross the road on my own.

Sometimes I think I could really be happy just being a DJ. Having my own radio show and playing all the records I love would be terrific – so long as I knew there were people listening.

I don't know what's there myself (speaking of himself). When people get too close, I shut them off.

Since I've been successful I've always laid myself fairly open. I mean, once you go to football matches and people chant really vile things about you, you can take anything. I couldn't be like Prince or somebody like Michael (Jackson). That's where they get their mystique from. But you can't run away from it. (1988)

I lost my sense of values. I didn't appreciate what people did for me. I even resented people wanting my autograph because I'd

Elton with Stevie Wonder.

forgotten what it was like to be on the other side of the fence. (1977)

There we were, staring at each other across the room, and for ages no-one introduced us. I think both of us were a little too shy to make the first move and say 'hello'. Eventually though, we got talking, or at least I did. *(Mohammed)* Ali seemed really shy and it was a while before he actually managed to say something. After that though, I suppose you could say we were fighting fit, because we didn't stop talking all night'.

All I set out to be is honest in everything I do, and I know that a lot of people believe that I have not been honest over the last two or three years. (1975)

A lot of people get involved with the wrong kind of people. Fortunately, I'm good at shutting people off. I'm very wary of people I meet because so many people are out to push themselves on you or push their drugs on you or something. I was pretty naïve before I came to America but that week made me grow up. I mean, that week I must have seen all the con men and hypsters and I found I could see through it all for the first time in my life and I pledged not to end up like them.

There were two things I could have done. I could either have shut myself away, become thoroughly miserable and ruined myself in the process but I realised how ridiculous it was to become a recluse.

I've also wanted to be good at wallpapering, I'm having my house done at the moment and I'm amazed at people putting up wallpaper, it's so skilful.

I'm relieved to be starting my life all over. When I've been on tour I've always had bodyguards with me because there was always some crank who wanted to beat me up or shoot me. I went from plane to hotel. I tried keeping in touch with everything going on in the world but whatever I did I felt more and more remote. (1977)

I had to do a lot of work to get honest. I had to get humble and lose my arrogance and self-pity, all those things that come from drink, drugs, and being excessive. In twenty-one months I turned my life around.

My God, it was like the heavens had opened up. I found for the first time in my life that I just couldn't cope. Like everyone else, I've had personal disasters which I took in my stride, but not everything all at once. I had nine months of everything going wrong. *(On his 'burn-out', 1987-88.)*

That's what I want to clear up *(that only Mick Jagger has been photographed at more parties)*; I don't usually go to parties, the only ones that I attend I get photographed at because people say, 'Oh look, there's Elton John'. I hate parties.

It annoys me when people think that I turn up everywhere. I don't go to many parties. How many British receptions have you seen me at? I hate parties. I can't bear them. I mean, I'll go if Rod's going 'cause he's my mate and if Taupin says he'll go then I'll go, or if it's someone I really admire.

Just the other night I forgot the words of 'Candle In The Wind'. If I was Rod Stewart, I'd have got the crowd to sing along and nobody would notice but I found it very embarrassing. At least it tells them - see I'm human.

I used to be afraid of many things. I wouldn't let anyone get close to me. As soon as that was happening I'd say 'enough' and clam up. But after endless touring I had a great rest period in Barbados last year. It taught me to relax, something I could never do. It was the turning point in my life. (1977)

A sing-song at home is great but if I'm doing my own material, I feel like I'm on trial. Most people would think I was showing off anyway, so I just can't be bothered. A concert is a completely different thing.

I'd like to be in comedy films. A film like Blazing Saddles, where you could laugh all the time. I've got a very sort of Monty Python-ish humour and don't know if I'd catch on in America. It's a little avant-garde.

I needed it, I'd been playing concerts all over America. One minute I'd be on the East Coast and the next I'd be on the West. Then 'way up North, or in Canada! I really began to get confused. So when I arrived in Los Angeles, I checked into this hotel and gave instructions not to be disturbed for a week. I hardly went out. I just sat around in bed, caught up with the news, read a few books. And I don't usually like relaxing.

Well, the money and success and fame are all very well but there was no balance, no balance in my life. We get one life to live on this earth and I'm not going to pontificate but I was wasting very precious time by just doing things that were making me into a miserable wretched human being. I was still loveable - obviously because people loved me enough to care about me - but, I couldn't love myself and there was no balance between the success and the personal life.

And I think everyone needs that simple thing. Everyone needs to be able to do things for themselves. When I went for treatment, in hospital, I was worried about being able to work the washing machine. I couldn't work a washing machine. You had to do your washing. It was pathetic. I was 42 and I couldn't work a washing machine and I couldn't do things for myself anymore. I didn't do the basic things that everybody should do really for themselves - do my own shopping, go out and just do things. I came out of treatment and went back to England and lived on my own for the first time in my life. I'd never lived on my own. I always grew up with the family or had people staying with me or everything. I bought a dog and I lived on my own and it was terrific. I had to do things for myself and gain self respect and function as everyone else on this planet. I was cared for too much. (1992)

There's a lot of people who are unhappy, but there's so many people with disorders of some kind, or addictions. It's hard to admit the breakdown and it's tough. But the greatest thing I learnt since I got sober was communication. I find it very easy to play before fifty-sixty thousand people but I found it very difficult to talk to someone one-to-one. I could do it on a talk show because it was my job, but in actual real life I would hide behind my glasses or my costumes and I would be very shy and I would need a drink to give me the courage to talk to somebody. I've learnt that that's not necessary or... I have to use the telephone to communicate with people and tell people how I'm feeling. (1992)

It's the most incredible experience I have ever had in my life. I mean - I've got my sense of values back, my mother and family back. She's moved back to England. She just lives 10 minutes away from me and I speak to her every day. My mother used to say, 'I don't want a diamond bracelet. I don't need another car. I just want a phone call from you just here and there.' I could never understand that because I was so self-centred and I was so in my own world. I thought. 'What's she talking about?' And of course, all a mother wants a son to do is to have a conversation with her, to be with her, to see her, take her to dinner, to spend some time with her. That's how my values had got lost. Now I've got them back, I've got my family back. (1992)

At one point in my life I would have felt ashamed to say this but I don't feel ashamed because I can't afford to take that shame around with me any more. I don't think it's a very good thing to do and I don't recommend it to anybody. It's got me to realise how precious this life is and how wonderful friends and family are and they are the most precious things. You mentioned money and you mentioned success and it's very nice but it's not what makes me happy and I'm glad to be able to admit that for me for the first time in my life. (1992)

Wit and Wisdom

My career is gonna be short... one and a half years, that's all.
I'll fade into obscurity.

Pop music is a game. And you must always treat it as a game.
It is very enjoyable if you are winning. And very miserable if you
are not.

She *(my mother)* didn't like the idea at all but I told her it was
too late to do anything about it. I'd grown fed up with people saying
'This is Elton John, but his real name is Reginald Kenneth Dwight'.
I figured some people might not want to call me Elton, so I picked
Hercules. I said to mum 'You can call me Herk, if you like, because
my middle name is now Hercules'. She nearly had a fit and said,
'Fancy calling yourself after Steptoe's horse.'

I think the thing about me is that I've managed to retain a sense
of humour about this whole game, and it is a game. It's a game that
fascinates me and I love it and being involved in it, because you never
know what's going to happen.

I think that Lennon said that records ought to come out the day
after you've finished them, and I feel the same way.

Oh hello Eric, here on your own are you?
*(to Eric Carmen, just after he'd reached number two in the US charts with
'All By Myself' in 1976.)*

I've never regarded pop music as an art form. I think it's just entertainment and I think that is why pop groups are coming back, because people are fed up with moodies and they'd rather go out and have a good time. (1972)

Look at it this way. I know people who have spent six months of their life going from hotel to hotel, suitcase to suitcase to save money. They're thoroughly miserable while they're doing it and they're thoroughly miserable at the end of it.

There was a review I had in the *Financial Times* once, which said I was an extremely funky pub pianist, and I thought that was a pretty good summing-up of what I am. (1973)

It's hard for a new band to get off the ground here. They have to flog themselves to death for two years before they have a chance and the prospect unnerves kids that might come in.

Sure I get some stick up North... don't sit down while Elton's around, or you'll get a penis up your arse... very nice when it's sung by 1,500 Halifax supporters and it echoes around the stadium. And I get people I'm with asking what they're singing and I reply, oh nothing... nothing. I can take all that until the cows come home.

Most of us who made it are 25–30 and we have a musical history, a knowledge of what went before.

I'm very much a legend man. I really like legends. That includes those who made their names, retired, and became recluses. People like Garbo, Mae West, Groucho are high on my list. So are departed stars like Noël Coward and Laurel and Hardy.

Elton and Rod Stewart during a concert at Watford Football Club.

I'm a tubby little singer and I can't understand why people scream for me. There must be a reason but God knows what it is.

I don't care if the critics write me off as concerned with only being popular. What's wrong with that?

It's beginning to be a problem, the fact that people expect me to walk out in seventy-five feet heels.

It's not embarrassing being a star, as long as you don't believe in it yourself. The trouble comes when you do, and then it all stops. It has all been unexpected, anyway.

Sex is much more liberal and blatant in America; there is no charade to go through. When we are on tour as a group we have fans in certain

Elton, Marc Bolan, Ringo Starr and Mickey Finn.

towns who always turn up to our parties and they'll try and make it with you. But the groupie girl as such is a dying art.

A single is possibly still the best way to get an act off the ground.

You have to realise you can only reach a certain peak. One day it's just going to tail off slightly, moderately, or heavily. I'm quite prepared for that to happen. You have to be prepared to do other things.

It's true that I'm a cuddly sort of person. Rod Stewart is the Tescos and I'm the Sainsburys of this business. He's rougher and might inspire earthier adoration. I suppose I'm more sedate. In the beginning I suppose it was a case of being in the right place at the right time. Things have always seemed to fit nicely into place in my life. Maybe there weren't that many singing piano players around.

It's a new generation of fans because it's eleven years since The Beatles and they don't want to know about The Beatles. They want their own heroes like The Osmonds or David Cassidy, but why pick on me or T. Rex or Slade?

Once I said I would retire within three years. That was five years ago.

At 60 I'll be a bald pub pianist playing 'Your Song' with people shouting for the latest Top 20 hits.

You can't afford to disappear for too long. People forget so easily.

I like the acclaim. We all like to be idolised. But I get a bit cheesed off with being called Wonderboy.

I didn't want to be a guy who went to university and ended up working as a gardener because he still didn't know what he wanted to do.

The Royals are really nice people and like any other family. You don't go up to them and say, 'Hello mate' or, 'Hello Fergie, how's your TV set?'.

Elton with Iggy Pop.

Success did take me by surprise. A few things had to be straightened out first though. Like when I went to the States, I was being introduced to people as a genius. I remember one incident at the Troubadour when I was actually introduced to Quincy Jones as a genius. I was so fucking embarrassed, I couldn't believe it. I apologised to him. I went mad at the guy who said it. I told him, never do that to me again. They do tend to go like that in America. But once I got my relationship sorted out with my PR bloke over there and told him to cool it, everything went very well. It was those four years that I humped my organ and amps down to the Cue Club that came in handy then. (1972)

Yes, I am joining the Stones. And so is Ronnie Bond of The Troggs.

I have worked bloody hard, and I pay my taxes. I never feel guilty. Just lucky, that's all. Bloody lucky.

The States is so big you can't get that kind of intimate feeling. You get big anonymous bands signed to big anonymous record labels turning out big anonymous music. I couldn't tell a member of Styx apart from a member of Boston.

I tell you what has ruined pop is all these fucking PRs and people like that. 'You can't do that, it'll ruin your image!' But it would be superb to do a package tour, a really bizarre one with Gary Glitter, David Bowie, Cassidy, The Who and make it really showbiz – if you did it for a week – could you imagine the lunatic things that would go on? It would just be insane. And wouldn't it be a great live album? (1973)

I haven't seen a decent film or heard a decent record that's come out of that part of the world *(Los Angeles)* for a long time... it's devoid of ideas, stale... it'll come back, it always has done.

Glitter rock was a bit predictable and rock and roll came back for
its annual visit and that pissed me off.

In any type of artistic venture, when you take something out of it,
you should contribute something to its advancement, too.

You encounter so many big bands who insist on travelling in
separate cars, have separate dressing rooms and stay in separate hotels.
What a hypocritical way to earn a living!

Look, they're all *(record companies)* very enthusiastic about putting out
their records on coloured vinyl or in a picture bag, but whose bill does
that come off – not the record company's.

I've got a fear of dying but there's got to be a record shop in heaven
somewhere.

I think the tension almost forces kids to get right into the music.
Apart from the general turmoil this was my other main impression.
Kids over there *(in the US)* really know about music.

I wouldn't pay 45/- for my own record. I would hope to get
a reduced price on my LP and sell the double set for the price of one.
I don't think people will figure it's a cheap label thing, because it's
a relatively unknown label anyway. I'm on DJM, but I hope it would
sell if it was on the Minnie Mouse label.

Everything I do is tongue in cheek and I enjoy it and that's why I enjoy the punk thing. It's wonderful. I'm five foot eight and hardly have any hair at all! Even I used to dye my eyebrows pink... and those stupid shoes I used to wear, they were monstrosities. But it was all fun.

God knows I helped to create that kind of thing, but I don't like it *(speaking of the music world being the domain of big businessmen and accountants)*. I read that people buy 12 million albums by an artist and I just can't comprehend those sort of figures. Record companies think in how many units they're selling. You pick up an American magazine and you'll see them bragging about it. They become a machine which doesn't have enough sensitivity.

In the old days, pop records weren't made because they sounded chic. It was done out of complete naïveté. Everything is done now for a motive. I was thinking the other day how nice it used to be to go to the Harrow Granada and see Larry Parnes spectacular or one of those shows, and I can never remember ever seeing any PA speaker. When you go to a concert now, you see masses of speakers, but on those package shows everything used to come through the house PAs. I suppose that's why I started my own record company to get back some of that simplicity.

I am still the ultimate music fan, but I feel the rock industry has become just that - an industry. I abhor it, especially as I was one of those who started it... becoming the first million dollar plus signing in

America complete with full-page advertisement in the New York Times and whatever. I was knocked out by it all at the time, very flattered, but who wouldn't be. People like, say, Kate Bush only come through once in a while – make a good single and sell lots of albums on the strength. But for every Kate Bush there are a hundred others who could use that money to boost their career in terms of promotion.

I can't see the point of having a nice house and keeping it empty. To me it's a home, a place to relax. When people call in I like them to feel relaxed and happy. When they do, I know the atmosphere is just the way I want it.

I saw a TV programme on Punk Rock and my initial reaction was 'Silly sods, bloody ridiculous going round with safety pins in them'. Then I thought I must be getting old though because that's the sort of thing my mother used to say to me about ten years ago. (1977)

What they (Americans) need over here is the British punk revolution. That's great music. (1978)

ton models the boots he wore to play the nball Wizard in the movie of Tommy.

I love America, but there is no way to describe the feeling you get when the plane touches down again in England. Within minutes you are back into a British environment. There is a great humour you get in Britain that you don't get anywhere else in the world. Even when there is a depression here people themselves don't get depressed. There may be no sugar, no bread and bombs going off everywhere but there is still no place like it. When I played in Canada one fan threw a Union Jack on stage. I have kept it and it's at home now. You always get emotional when you see the British flag or when you meet Britons abroad.

I think the secret of life is to have a good time – and to give other people a good time, too! To enjoy what you're doing, to have good friends, and to fall in love are all parts of it. If you keep these things in mind, you'll make out all right.

I'm all against most of the people at EMI and Decca who earn money out of music without being really interested. I've always been very lucky with DJM. It's a small company where you can go in and say what you want and it's like a home and a family.

My career is the only tangible asset, the only thing left to cling to.

I'm only bloody 39. I've got a lot of livin' to do yet. I'll wait until I've got one foot in the grave before I'll publish, and anyway she will not be writing my autobiography. I will be doing it. (On the reported offer by Mrs. Thatcher's daughter, Carol, to write his story.)

Sex, Love and Relationships

In this day and age saying you're bisexual is no big deal.

I've been fortunate. I've been surrounded by good people.
I haven't ended up bitter and twisted like some artists, because they went through too many bad deals. My friends haven't become my enemies. With the passing years we can still trust each other.
I'm happy that I've pleased people, I'm happy that I'm going to be around for a long time. I don't think about growing old, that would be boring.

I have a close circle of friends who just aren't in the public eye – sort of like Elvis and his... motorbike people. They were people who first gave Bernie and me encouragement. It's very much a family. That's why it's so incestuous sometimes. We've still got the same roadies, and the guy who mixes our sound, and our agent Howard Rose and Connie, and I like it that way. I'm sort of like – not Godfather – but everything around is incestuous, and that's probably why there might be a lot of talk about us.

Opposite Page:
Elton as Tina Turner.

Top: Elton with Melanie Green.

The great thing about the whole Elton John set-up is everyone is so happy doing what they're doing. We all know that the moment anyone is unhappy then they can pull out. That's what we told Paul *(Buckmaster)* and Gus *(Dudgeon)* when we first asked them to join in. (1971)

People do change towards you. There's that attitude that, 'It's all right for you, you're earning money'. They automatically harden and you do wish you could be accepted by your old mates. But, sadly, with very few exceptions you lose contact. You change, they change. Resentment creeps in. And it gets to the point where it's too late to patch it up or try to get back and say, 'Look I haven't seen you for six years but how've you been doing?' And they've got a mortgage and two kids and you're sitting there with the Rolls outside.

Her name was Nellie, and she had long blonde hair – dyed, I think. She lived in a caravan that got moved on by the police every few weeks. When I went there, it was 'turn left at the third field in Southall'. The caravan was the cleanest thing I have ever seen in my life. Her parents were great. Nellie was 20, much older than I was. People have got the wrong idea about gypsies. She was fantastic, with a great sense of humour. I would never want to be a gypsy. *(On an early girlfriend when Elton was only 15.)*

When I lived with her *(an early girlfriend)* she used to beat me up. I couldn't understand it. But we got this flat in Islington and for six months I was in love and idyllically happy. But I was under her thumb, as it were, and she hated my music and wanted to marry me. My mother and Bernie thought I was mad. But because it was the first relationship of my life I defended it and clung to it. When you're

wrong there's nothing worse than somebody else telling you so.
If you actually know you're wrong and nobody says it, you
can own up easier. (1975)

I've seen so many musicians' marriages going through difficulties
on the road. You can't take your old lady with you all the time because
it's a bore, and you want a little bit of freedom - that's a rock'n'roll
musician's outlook on life. So I don't want to get settled down yet.
(1975)

I'm not your actual sex idol, am I?

It was a narrow escape. But if the marriage had proceeded it
would have been the ruination of me. It would have impeded my
career. I was so relieved when it was off; it was as though someone

had saved my life. Of course I felt for her. But what could I do? Would she have suffered an unhappy marriage?

I find it far easier to get to know ladies in America. English ladies put up so many fronts. American ladies are very bold, and that breaks the ice for me. I can never say boo to a goose to anybody. I'm very shy and I need somebody to help me out.

My sex life? Um, I haven't met anybody I would like to have any big scenes with. It's strange that I haven't. I know everyone should have a certain amount of sex and I do, but that's it and I desperately would like to have an affair. I crave to be loved. That's the part of my life I want to have come together in the next two or three years. And it's partly why I'm quitting the road. My life in the last six years has been a Disney film and I have to have a *person* in my life. I have to. Let me be brutally honest about myself. I get depressed easily. Very bad moods. I don't think anyone knows the real me. I don't even think I do. I don't know what I want to be exactly. I'm just going through a stage where any sign of affection would be welcome on a sexual level. I'd rather fall in love with a woman eventually because I think a woman probably lasts much longer than a man, but I really don't know. I've never talked about this before. But I'm not going to turn off the tape. I haven't met anybody that I would like to settle down with of either sex. (1976)

There's nothing wrong with going to bed with someone of your own sex. I think everybody is bisexual to a certain degree. I don't think it's just me. It's not a bad thing to be. I think you're bisexual. I think everybody is. (1976)

It's going to be terrible with my football club. It's so hetero, it's unbelievable but I mean... who cares? I just think people should be very free with sex. They should draw the line at goats. (1976)

Everybody thinks we *(Bernie and Elton)* were *(lovers)*, but we weren't, but if we had been I don't think we would have lasted so long. The press probably thought John Reid and I were having an affair, but there's never been a serious person the whole time, nobody really. (1976)

Nobody's had the balls to ask me about it before. I would have said something all along if someone had asked me, but I'm not going to come out and say something just to be... I do think my personal life should be personal. I don't want to shove it over the front pages like some people I could mention. To be on the front pages with my tongue down someone's throat. That's really appalling. I'd like to have some children but I don't know if the time is right. (1976)

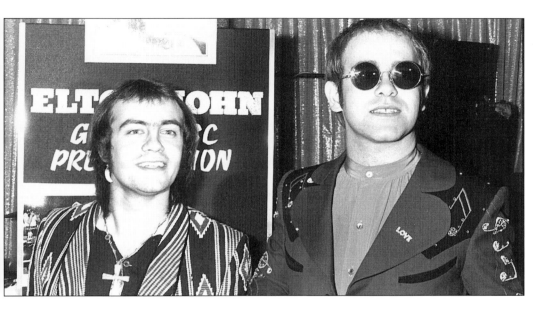

I have no regrets about saying it *(that he was bisexual)*. It was just a relief. It's not as if I'm a child molester. The statement has had no effect on my life. I haven't even had any bad letters. (1977)

It's not a romance, just a friendship. She is a very good friend of mine. She lives in Monte Carlo and came over to England to see my concerts at the Rainbow in London. *(Speaking of Melanie Greene, at one time rumoured to be Elton's special girl.)*

My sex life at 30 is satisfactory. I mean not once a day. Say three times a week... at least. And more female than male. My dream type is the vastly experienced woman who knows everything about the world.

I never want to be a dad. Once you sit next to a bawling child on a plane you realise you can't cope.

It's more or less impossible for me to have a personal relationship with someone because I don't want to change anyone's life-style. But if they are involved with me then they have to make concessions and they have to change. I like being alone and yet I crave for someone to love. It's really a tortured existence. I don't have anyone at the moment.

I don't fall in love that easy. I haven't had much of a chance. With fans you have to be very careful. You are leading yourself into a dangerous situation if you play with their emotions. Some fans really think you are in love with them and haven't even met you.

It's accepted that there are a lot of gay people in the theatrical profession – but I just wish that those people who represent the gay movement would send themselves up just once on TV.

A gay person is invariably regarded as a child molester... someone who hangs around in public toilets and is a filthy and utterly depraved human being. Well, that's not the case at all, because when you check out the number of sexual assaults in the courts the majority involve heterosexuals.

Some of my best friends are women – particularly older women. I find younger women a bit shallow. They're too concerned with money and possessions.

I like women just as much as I like men because I like human beings. They are more compassionate, and I find them cleverer. Who knows, one day perhaps I will have a family.

Bisexuality would not be in the way of marital bliss – the sort of woman I'd marry would understand that anyway.

I've never slept with a fan. It would be very dangerous, very harmful, and could totally louse up their lives. No way – it's unfair.

Everyone knows I'm desperately in love with Miss Piggy. I'm doing a TV show in America, but she will not be my guest because I gather she is signed up by The Muppets. So I haven't mentioned it to her. Kermit explained to me that she can be impulsive and pigheaded – and if I invited her on the show and she broke her contract all hell would break loose.

I only became aware that I was bisexual in 1970. It was a bit of a surprise. Before that I was heterosexual. I know which way I'd rather go. I would rather have a wife and children. That's one of the things I would really like to do.

Top: Elton with Jennifer Rush.

Bottom: With Cher.

I find it extremely hard to say things to a girl. I'm just not romantic.
If I'm going out with a girl, I'll buy her things. But... I can't *say* things!

I'm looking now for the right girl. I'll probably pick someone
who works behind the counter at Woolworth's or Marks and Spencer's,
where I go to buy my pants. I shall need to be careful. No playboy
types for me. Most of them are out to get themselves a mink coat and
a big diamond ring. I'd want to live with her first, because that's the
only way to get to know and understand her. And I don't think it's
necessarily true that the girl would get the worst of the deal, because
she would also have the chance of ending the relationship before
marriage. Long engagements aren't that important. I know some
couples who have to save up for maybe five years. That wouldn't
apply to me.

I would rather have a wife and children, because I adore children,
that's one of the things I would really love to do. I'll be 30 on March
25 and I'm quite looking forward to it. It's like I've forgotten Elton
John I and Elton John II is starting now. I think that's the only way
to go about things.

I had everything but I had nothing. I needed the challenge of change
in my life, making it more fulfilled and sharing. The only thing missing
for my life was a wife and family. I could see myself ending up as an
eccentric, living alone, and being incredibly fussy. Rather like
Quentin Crisp, except that I dust and he doesn't.

Elton with his wife Renate.

Elton and Renate on their wedding day on February 24, 1984, in Sydney.

The house is very much all my own doing and desires, it was very much a man's house. Renate is taking over and making it more of a home than it was before. We are known as the odd couple which is fair enough because I made a statement in the 1970s that I was bisexual.

I don't get my own way all the time any more but it's nice to come home and actually share things. *(On marriage with Renate.)*

I never really had any thought of getting married. It's ridiculous but suddenly, bang! After 37 years I found someone I wanted to marry. Mind you, I never cast anything out of my mind. I believe you create your own luck and if you are very positive in your thinking, something will happen. Suddenly it had and I knew it was the right thing to do. I'm so happy and very much in love. (1984)

We are trying for children. It just hasn't happened yet. But maybe that's a good thing for the moment because I am so busy touring. I'd just like to have children and I don't mind whether it's a boy or a girl. I simply want to be a family man – and I'm not getting any younger. I was an only child and I didn't like that very much. Ideally I'd like to have two but you never know.

Our marriage is strong and getting stronger. *(EJ on his marriage to Renate 1986.)*

I know a lot of people have said my marriage is a definite cover up, and that I only got married to be proper. But that's just idle gossip. In truth, though I admitted publicly I was gay once, I never ruled out the possibility of getting married. But I'd like to have a child when we can spend some time with it. (1986)

I gave it my best shot, and certainly it's not Renate's fault. I feel this terrible guilt. She is so supportive when things are going badly for me.

I miss not seeing my wife any more.

In 1988 Elton successfully sued The Sun newspaper for damages after they printed untrue stories about his sex life...
They can say I'm a fat old sod, they can say I'm an untalented bastard, they can call me a poof, but they mustn't lie about me. (1987)

Obviously I wish it had never happened. It didn't just affect me. It affected everybody who worked with me. They didn't know what to believe. My mother moved to Spain to get away from it all. The worst part of it was that the people who sold those stories were supposed to have been my friends. It taught me a lot about the value of real friendships. I learned who my real friends are. (1989)

If I had just run away from it all, it would have looked as if I really was guilty, and I'd have been deserting all the people who stuck by me. Eventually I got what I wanted from *The Sun* and in a strange way I think the experience has made me a stronger person. (1989)

I have been vindicated. I don't think it's any of the judge's business. *(After winning his case against The Sun but at the same time being rebuked by the judge.)*

I feel very relieved. It was embarrassing and depressing. I just want to get on with my life, now that I have been vindicated.

This is the best Christmas present I could wish for. Life is too short to bear grudges and I don't bear *The Sun* any malice.

Diets & Health

This has really shaken me. When you're used to working non-stop tours across the States and so on you start to think you're superhuman. Then something like this happens and you realise you're not. *(Speaking of the time when it was thought he might have had a heart attack.)*

I had terrible pains in my chest, arms and legs. I couldn't breathe. I could hardly move for the pain. But I managed to stagger to my personal assistant's room – and he took one look at me and called the doctor.

As I went down I said to myself 'Hello this is it. The Grand Heart, then out you go!' The first came this summer. I fell over on the tennis court and couldn't get up. They had to get a wheel chair for me and push me back into the house. *(Telling the media that he had two major physical upsets.)*

If I look at a doughnut I put on two pounds without even eating it. It's not as if I am Jagger or Bowie. I don't have to get really physical. I can just sit behind my piano and pretend I am Ray Charles. I am his weight.

The biggest fear of my life is going blind or deaf. Deafness, in fact, would be worst of all, because without sound I would have no music. God, the thought of it. Complete blank. Complete, eternal silence.

There are certain things I have to avoid at all costs. I mean, I'd enjoy having a plate of sandwiches for supper, sometimes! But I've only got to glance at a sliced loaf to put on pounds! So I steer clear. I'd rather miss out on some of the foods I like, than get fat. My tennis helps to keep my weight down, too. Sport is great from that point of view. Mind you, I must be honest. I can weaken at times. You see, I love Indian food and when I get a craving for a nice hot curry I have to have one. That's my biggest weakness!

I just love to go down to the village and do my own shopping. I don't cook badly, but I don't really call myself a cook. I like roast lamb, roast beef – that sort of thing. Funnily enough, most people I know are vegetarians. I'm very traditional when it comes to the type of thing I like, although I enjoy Indian food. I love all this shopping business, especially in the local butcher's. Everybody around here knows what I do and they're very nice to me. *(Having moved to the Wentworth Estate near Virginia Water.)*

I have lost more than 28lb and I'm down to under 11 stone. I can't wait to see how I look in another six months. (1987)

With John Peel.

I'm staying in Australia for an operation on my throat. I'm scared. I'm so damned scared. *(After a growth had been found on his vocal cords in 1986.)*

Sometimes I like beans on toast. Funny really isn't it? But just because you move into a big house and all that, you don't change your ways. Or, at least, I haven't.

I absolutely love *(chocolate)*, especially straight from the fridge – there's nothing like it. Once I start eating I can't really stop. But I'm not quite as bad as Renate, she is a total chocoloholic. (1988)

Drugs & Alcohol

The trouble is I don't smoke or take pills or anything. Some of these people get very upset when they offer me a joint and I say no thanks. (1973).

I was drinking about a pint of whisky a day, and it was so easy to get into. I've given up drinking spirits. (1974)

I simply gave up all forms of alcohol – I drink Perrier all the time now – and most forms of carbohydrates. It was a bit restricting, because I really love things like chips and rice pudding and hamburgers, but definitely worth it. *(Speaking about the time when he lost 37lb in just 13 weeks.)*

I've seen what cocaine can do to people. And hash just gives me a headache, although they get a bit funny in America when I refuse a joint. And groupies... well, I'm not really interested in one night stands.

I think drugs – I'm not talking about marijuana which I tried once, and passed out – are potentially very dangerous.

I know alcohol is just as bad as drugs and unfortunately I drink too much. Being involved with a football club you tend to drink a lot of whisky – so I'm trying to cut down.

At one point early this year I started drinking vodka Martinis. I was practically addicted to them. You're supposed to sip them but I'm an all or nothing person and I just used to whoosh them down.

I got to the stage where I was drinking 10 to 18 Martinis a day.
I would need three or four before I went out in the evening.
Then I'd go on to red wine. I thought I was having a great time.
I felt great, the life and soul of the party. (1988)

I've got lots of friends who've gone to Alcoholics Anonymous and
each has become a better person for it. But I did it on my own, the
way I've always had to solve things. (1988)

I've made a lot of mistakes in my life, and I've done a lot of things
I regret, that I can be ashamed of. Most people have skeletons in their
closets but I would not advise people to take drugs. I can't stop
anyone taking drugs, because I took a lot of drugs, and I drank a lot...
I missed so much by taking drugs... but I am so happy about actually –
being alive. (1992)

I had a very rough time. It's all straightened out. I've been straight and
sober for two and a half years, no, two years and one month. (1992)

I went to hospital, in Chicago. I had an eating disorder, I was
bulimic, I was a drug addict and I was an alcoholic. And that was all
at once. I was isolated in my room. I was very obese and I was very
unhappy and yet I wouldn't ask anybody to help me out. I knew I had
a problem; you didn't have to be a magician to know I had a serious
problem in my life. But I thought that asking for help or admitting
that I have... I always thought I could solve things on my own.
I equated being a success as an artist as being a successful man
monetarily... that you could solve all your own problems. Of course,
there's no logic really behind that. But the ego gets in the way and
the paranoia and everything that comes with doing those stupid things.
And I did them to the extremes, and I suffered for it. And in the end
I managed to say... you know the pilot light inside a gas oven or
something like that, well mine was about that big, when I said yes
I wanted to get well. I'll ask for help, I'll go away and I'll live again
because I really felt as if I was dead anyway. I was like a carcass that
was shifted around. I just got up in the morning, showered, I got put
into a car, on to a plane, on to a stage – a bit like Elvis Presley, very
much so, very similar and it's a shame. Your pride, a very false pride
to have, too proud to ask for help, thought it was a sign of weakness
and of course, it was the best thing I ever did. As soon as I asked for
help the old pilot light shot back up. I wanted to live, I wanted my
life back, I wanted my dignity back and I wanted my self respect back
and I'd lost it. I'd lost my mother. My mother had moved to Spain.
She didn't want to be anywhere near me. And it's sad when that
happens. I was very lonely. I had wonderful friends, and people
who would tell me these things that I should do something but I,
of course, wouldn't listen. (1922)

Clothes & Accessories

In my early days I had long hair, a Zapata moustache, and a taste for bright clothes. I wore shorts colourfully adorned by Noddy, which had been made from nursery curtain material from a friend.

Yes, I had this outfit designed with wooden trousers. It wasn't very successful. Not very good for moving about, I'm afraid. I wasn't going to wear them through the whole set, and underneath would be a pair of normal trousers. And there were supposed to be mock birds which would fly out. But as I said it didn't exactly work!

I usually have at least one catastrophe when getting dressed. Tonight it is the bow tie. My pale blue with yellow spots falls apart due to the catch coming off. I have to choose another. I find that I have a very hard time relaxing, and my favourite occupation, when I'm not doing any of the aforementioned *(performing, recording, on the road)* is to lie back and watch TV and just tune out.

Somewhere at home I've 179 pairs of glasses scattered around in drawers. I used to hide behind them, sitting in a little corner and feeling safe because it stopped people seeing how frightened I really was.

I've got some Noddy shirts. They're made out of nursery curtain material. A neighbour made them for me. She has a boutique in Ealing, and she plasters the walls with posters of us which is very kind... I'm always being recognised in Ealing!

One of the critics says I look like an albino baboon but I prefer to think I look like a human cheesecake. I have been forced to alter my stage image. That glittery suit business has been overdone by other people. I shall go on stage now in evening dress.

My stage clothes put me in the right mood for a performance. Without them I just wouldn't feel like Elton John at all.

People knock me for wearing tailed pink lamé suits that glitter and those insane platform shoes and the whole electric Liberace bit. And they're really going to groan when they see my new glasses that cost $5,000 each and which light up. I can't believe they take it seriously.

The clothes thing is very me, psychologically speaking.

When you're fat you can't buy nice clothes and today I'm probably rebelling against that.

Why did I wear those platforms? Just for a laugh. It gives the audience a giggle. But the real reason goes deeper. Perhaps it started when I was a kid, my dad was strict and I had to wear dull clothes. Soon as I got the chance, I went to the other extreme. If I'd had more freedom as a kid, I might be wearing smart suits today. (1971)

I'd also like to get into funny things like padded suits. You see, I haven't really got the sexiest body in the world so I like to have comedy in my act.

Elton with Noel Edmonds.

I've been throwing clothes out and thinking 'Did I wear that?' It's like high-heeled shoes - I wouldn't wear anything else, and I couldn't envisage the day that I didn't, but I think I'm not going to now. (1973).

Those Lurex suits are going. I'm having designers design a whole lot more for me now because I'm bored with tail suits. I've had them for ages. There's no limit to what I can wear on stage, but it's all tongue in cheek.

I cornered the market in platform shoes. That has to be the worst era of fashion ever I would've thought, and I have some of the prime worst examples. The higher they went, the higher I used to get them. When I first joined the football club I was six foot two. (1988)

I did not buy £13,000 worth of fur coats for this tour and indeed have not worn a fur coat on any part of the tour. *(Replying to animal lovers when members of the Animal Activists distributed leaflets to fans outside the Theatre Royal, Drury Lane, where Elton was performing. They claimed the star had spent £13,000 on furs.)* I object to these people getting publicity by giving away leaflets outside my concerts.

I feel it is a new era, hence I've taken to wearing contact lenses. I've lost a lot of weight and I've had a hair transplant. (1978)

Elton with Liz Taylor.

Hair

Anyone would think I was the only guy to have a hair transplant in the 20th century.

Looking at it now I think it was all worthwhile. I had the operation in Paris and there's two more to go before it's finished. It's pure vanity. *(Talking about his hair transplant treatment, the moment when after two years he removed his hat!)*

I don't want to go bald, and I certainly wasn't going to wear an Irish jig. So I had to look for another way out. (1979)

I'm having a third transplant in Paris on Wednesday. I'm told there will be twice as much on top as there is now. It doesn't hurt a bit while it's being done, but it isn't half tender afterwards.

I just wanted to see what it would look like to have green hair. I wanted to dye it green all over but decided that might be too horrendous.

I was anaesthetised for five hours while hair was taken from the back of my head and put on the front. It's all 100 per cent vanity. But I'm thrilled with the result.

It's taken a long time. I'm sure people were beginning to think nothing was happening under my cap.

I feel younger. It's so easy to look younger when you've got hair, and that's just being honest. It takes 20 years off you *(speaking in 1992)*.

Politics

The world's destroying itself.

It's nonsense to make music and sport a political issue.
The only way I can improve things in the world is by going and
playing music. Nobody is going to tell me that I can't go anywhere
and have a look for myself. I don't want to be told what places are like.
I want to see the facts for myself. When I went to Russia I couldn't
believe how much like the Americans they were; the actual people
on the street were as warm and friendly as the Americans are.
And I wouldn't have thought that until I'd gone there. And nobody
is going to tell me that I can't go to South Africa when we have people
in the English cricket team who are South Africans. That is hypocrisy
beyond belief. I'll fight that.

I see people living in towns like Newcastle, Birmingham,
Manchester, Glasgow in the same squalid conditions they've lived in
for years. It's not right.

The Conservative Party has the principle that if you give the
people crap they have to accept it. I don't agree with that. I don't
know if they've heard of Watford in Russia but they soon will.
They will probably get fed up with hearing how good we are.
The British can be obsessed with trivia. I get really annoyed when
people keep asking me to take my cap off so they can have a look.
I feel like replying 'Okay, now you drop your drawers'. I am fed up
with both parties, really, but would never vote Tory. I am not going
to say who I am voting for though. I don't think that politics in music
ever had much of an effect. Look at all the singers in the Sixties
who tried to change the world through words. Life continued
much the same.

Elton and John Major.

I think National Music Day is a rather silly idea. I certainly want nothing to do with it. *(1992, in response to some claims that his concert with Eric Clapton had some reference to NMD.)*

I think there is such a lack of manners in the world today – and so much intolerance.

I'm against bigotry and prejudice and persecution. But if that stopped me playing music I would not play here because of the National Front or in the US because of the campaign against homosexuality.

I would not live in America for £100 a minute. We have enough trouble here with our soccer violence, but at least people don't walk the streets with guns. If young people could buy guns in supermarkets as they do in the States, we would have fans shot dead at Saturday matches.

I would never go back *(to Russia)* under the present circumstances, they hadn't invaded Afghanistan then. I can't help feeling it would have been better if the athletes hadn't gone. I'm a sports fanatic and loved Coe and Ovett's performances.

I think the Royal Family is one of Britain's greatest assets. I did a concert once in the grounds of Windsor Castle.

The music business is fantastic for breaking down barriers, and it's a pity this didn't spread wider. I don't like racial prejudice or any other form of intolerance.

Elton with Princess Alexandra.

I'm seeing a lot of people dying from AIDS, and I don't like bigotry, no matter what you've been born with. I think everyone deserves love and respect.

I resent the English press. I really don't like them. They're a bunch of liars, and for me they're the scum of the earth. *(Speaking after reading an editorial in a British newspaper post-Freddie Mercury Tribute concert that had as its focus the view that only homosexuals and drug-users get AIDS.)*

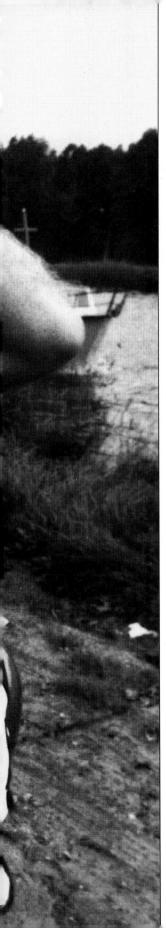

Money & Possessions

I have a financier who looks after the whole deal. I just go out there and play. I'm not interested.

I'm going to be a very rich boy. *(As he set off to tour the States, following upon the big hit single 'Your Song'.)*

I set out to cover the walls of my house with paintings. And I seem to have succeeded.

There was acre upon acre of land, a lot of it for grazing, and a herd of cattle too. In fact the cows produced the milk which was sent to the local dairy and then delivered to the front door. Crazy, huh? There was a stable too. But the fact is that the house was too large for me and Mum. It would have needed a whole team of people to look after it, keep it clean, turn out the stables, and so on. I'd have a payroll like the Royal Family.

I also decided that, despite the tax man's big axe, I am going to stay in England. I could never leave my job as a director of Watford Football Club, or my friendly neighbours like my old mate Rod Stewart.

I collect magazines – things like *The History Of World War II* in 96 volumes, and every one of the *Master Painter* series. At one time I collected cacti.

I am interested if someone is going to con me out of my money which I've earned through song writing or record royalties. But I've earned a lot of money. I'm probably a dollar millionaire, but I won't see any of it for ten years. Who needs it. I've got a place to live and a car, and that's all I need. Most important, I've had the opportunity to do what I want and get paid for doing it, and that's the greatest thing. All I've got left now is a grand piano and two paintings.

I gave my manager John Reid a white Rolls-Royce for Christmas. I bought my mother some valuable paintings and a £30,000 home. The nice thing about having money is being able to go into a fashionable store in jeans – tailored ones of course! – and order more or less anything you fancy. It eliminates a lot of hurdles.

I've got this record library at home and I fancy myself as an amateur disc jockey. I catalogue everything in my collection: cross

filed and everything! I'm a terrible collector of things. That's what I call my Liberace ring *(pointing to the little finger of his left hand)*. It was bought at Cartier as a present for me and it's made of gold and diamonds. It's sparkly and it's fun!

One of my prize pieces is a set of special spectacles which was given to me by those great guys in The Four Seasons. In fact, Franki Valli made a special visit to come and give me the present himself, and when I opened it, I could see why! There were four pairs of spectacles and across the lenses of each pair was painted a scene portraying one of the four seasons. Autumn, Summer, Winter and Spring. It absolutely knocked me out because they'd been specially designed for me. The most valuable pair I own is made of solid gold, but I'm so afraid of losing them that they're strictly for my eyes only.

I never imagined the whole thing would get so out of hand, so big. All this money, it's so silly, really.

I must have over 50,000 albums *(in 1978)* – is that a record? And God knows how many singles. They are kept in special libraries. In fact, the first room I had built on to my house when I bought it was a record library. The rest of it was really tacky but the records were most important.

Well, I suppose I do have a few. I have been buying them for years *(speaking about his love for jewellery)*. I love collecting things and I don't care whether they're things that increase in value or not. Whether they're priceless or a load of old rubbish. If I like them, I'll buy them. I know people think old dolls are a bit odd but I love them.

The only thing pop stars are interested in today is money.

It even has its own vineyard – large enough to produce sufficient wine for an entire year's drinking. This was one factor which persuaded wine connoisseur Elton to pay £400,000 for the house and 37 acres. *(About the new Berkshire mansion that he bought.)*

I hope I'm not part of a machine. Yes, I have a comfortable house, but let no-one fool you – every musician wants his just deserts. There are some who even want cash in hand before they go on stage. I've worked hard for the success I've had, so I think I deserve some reward. I can see nothing wrong in that.

I don't even own a wallet these days. I do have a little card case for credit cards but I never carry that either. (1980)

I don't spend as much money as I used to. It used to be Rembrandts for Christmas for friends, which was a bit stupid. I don't have any investments at all. Just my house and my collections. I did once buy a few shares on a friend's advice. A week later they went down by 30p and they've never shown any sign of recovering. So much for grand finance. (1980)

Everyone who is a major star in this country has been told to get out by their accountants and lawyers. I think a lot of people would stop being people and become companies. Just think, Cilla Black could become Cilla Cement Industries!

I suppose one secret of my success is that I have sensible people looking after me. Accountants who give me a good talking to when I spend too much money.

I don't want a yacht. I think they're boring. I wouldn't mind a helicopter. But I don't think I could afford one. Well, I suppose I could but the accountant would moan.

I'm a dreadful hoarder of things. I don't think I'll ever change.

I'd be really happy to have my own record shop... my idea of happiness would be to stand behind the counter at a place like Tower Records in Los Angeles to see what people bought. I used to do it at Musicland when 'Empty Sky' was out, and it fascinates me. I'd also like to have my own radio station so I could play some decent music.

I can find something to buy anywhere in the world, and I suffered from shipping disease. Only I could buy a tram in Melbourne and have

it shipped home. Then a lot of stuff was bought at auctions, which I never went to, because my hand would be permanently up. I've always instinctively bought stuff. Whether it's been a bad investment or a good investment, I've never really bought like that.

I never know what I'm going to buy. That was the whole great thing about it. I never knew what I wanted. I didn't go out for a certain set thing. I'd just suddenly find things I really liked. That was the whole joy about shopping for me. It was like an adventure. I bought on impulse. I live my life on impulse really. Always have. When I'm happy, I've always been like that. (1988)

I enjoy being wealthy. So many people are miserable with their success. But I don't think anything can bring fulfilment like being 100 per cent happy and having peace of mind. I've been fortunate. I haven't been ripped off that much. I've got the same people around me that I've had for years - the same roadies, the same management. Tremendous loyalty, and Watford, has taught me to be a better loser. (1984)

It does seem unreal that I can earn so much money because I come from a working class background. But I have no feelings of guilt about it.

Yes, I do enjoy money, because tomorrow night I might be knocked down by a No. 13 bus going to Walthamstow. If I'm successful I might as well enjoy it... if tomorrow suddenly my records stopped selling, I could get a gig at a record company promoting other artists' records. (1975)

You can't be a slave to music. I have all the things money can buy.

I can't imagine going to live in Geneva. There's nothing there but people who've gone to Geneva.

Elton with Bernie Taupin, John Reid, Les Bider and other executives from Warner Chappell shortly after signing a new £26 million music publishing deal with Warner Chappell Music at the opening of their new offices 1992.

I've always been told not to gamble.
(After watching the Grand National and not winning!)

I have worked very hard to get myself into the position that
I am in now. If people are prepared to pay that kind of money to see
me play then they will pay it. Anyway, most of it goes to the English
tax man. Sure I'm earning more than a doctor or a nurse but then
I'm paying more to help bail out this country - and I think people
tend to forget that a lot of the time.

My theory about spending money is that life is short. I could walk
out of a hotel room and the maid could come up to me and suffocate
me with a great big blanket and I'd be dead! The nicest thing about
my having money is that I love giving things. If I'm visiting a friend
I always take over a little something - even if it's only a bottle of
champagne or some flowers.

I'm just spreading a bit of happiness. I get a kick out of
giving presents, and I don't care if people call me Mr Moneybags.
I can't understand performers going into those deep depressions and
not wanting to do anything for a couple of years. It's all down to the
people you're involved with, I think. If you don't have a friend to
help you out, it just gets worse and worse.

I have installed a telex and I have got rid of all the phones in my
house. I haven't got a phone any more. If people want to get in touch
with me they can ring through a message to my office in Mayfair and
they will relay it to me. I've got little lights all over the house which
switch on when the telex machine is working. So I can go and read
it as it's coming over. Then I can call people back later.

Fame

I always wanted to be famous – the old ego bit. I never wanted to be
a movie star, because in fifty years' time if you mention an old film star's
name, they'll just say 'Who?' But they'll still be playing Gershwin.

I suppose I am a success. I never realised it until I went back to my
old school, Pinner Grammar, to do a concert the other month. I went
and looked at my old classroom and all the masters who taught me
were there and they were very nice and they just said 'Well, you've
done well. You've got on'. They looked just the same and I thought,
'What will they think of my act?' because it was a bit wild. But they
were all really nice. And then I drove away and thought, 'You've
made it. You've arrived'. It was a nice feeling.

I know a lot of stars who don't get enjoyment from fame and
are really miserable.

In the end John Reid phoned and I didn't believe it was him.
I kept asking what he looked like, what colour his hair was, how tall
was he? He thought I'd gone crazy and maybe I had by then.
(During Elton's LA visit and the accompanying hysteria.)

When you get plagued by autograph hunters and you are right in
the middle of a meal – that's a bit of aggravation.

It's lonely at the top.

We don't carry round a heavy mob, and if the stage is low we
have to watch out for them. It took us an hour to get out of a building
in Glasgow, and we've had to use decoys because we were trapped.
There were times when I thought the fans would rip us apart.
I'd rather they lined up in a line for two hours and I signed autographs
for them, but they wouldn't do that. I just don't know what it takes

for a girl to get it into her head that she must touch me. To be on stage and see some sixteen stone girl hurtling towards you is a frightening sight. When they grab hold of you it takes about six guys to get them off stage. It's amazing, but that's the only thing you can do because they're so strong.

I'm the sort of person who'll say yes to things a year in advance, and then when it comes round I'll think 'Fuck, I don't wanna do that'. I've been told I've got to calm down on decisions, be told what to do for a change. (1974)

One day I was sitting in the lounge, having a snooze on the couch when suddenly I woke up to find two girls just standing in front of me, staring at me. It really frightened me. They'd just walked in. I wouldn't have minded if they'd knocked on the front door, but it was really weird to wake up and see them. Anyway I showed them around the house and off they went quite happily.

I should think there have been more lies perpetuated about me than anyone else. All right, so I was an outlandish character, but there have been so many inaccuracies about me.

These days I never seem to have time to do the things I used to enjoy. It's rather saddening, especially losing contact with friends. I intend to put all that right in the years to come. I used to go out and buy the first things I saw. I don't do that now. You can only do so much with money. I have got a bit though. It's important to me how I look.

Over the past years I've been protected like the Crown Jewels. And it's funny because originally I just hoped to be a songwriter at Dick James Music earning £30 a week.

I'm glad things didn't go smoothly. If I had had a hit straight after leaving Bluesology, I'd be unbearable.

I got one hell of a kick just from hearing one of our songs on the radio and that's the way it should be.

I stopped doing interviews mainly because I didn't have much to say, not because we were over-exposed in the press. So because we weren't in the press so much, everyone sort of thought we were on the way out. I think 'Honky Château' has proved that the interviews aren't essential.

It was hard to think of anything to say to the bloody pavement. *(After being awarded the traditional Hollywood accolade of the star cut into the pavement. It was also the first time in 1,662 ceremonies that the street was closed due to so many people being present.)*

Top: Elton with Debbie Gibson and Billy Joel.

Above: With Sylvester Stallone.

I get a bit annoyed when people who don't know any better suggest I achieved fame easily. I've had my fill of slogging it out up and down motorways in an old battered van, eating any old food in transport caffs and wondering whether I would ever be anything but broke. But I didn't care. I knew of the many famous performers who had to go through times before reaching the top. Sure you get excited by your own success. I know a lot of artists say they never look at the charts, but that's nonsense. They're on the phone all the time. What's the point of recording something if you don't want to know how it's going? It's great having a number one record. Don't let anyone tell you it isn't. But that doesn't mean you're satisfied. All you have to do is see somebody on television you really like and you start thinking 'God, I wish I could play like that'. There's always something to strive for... A lot of people just don't have any ambition any more. It's just 'Oh well, it's time to tour again. Let's go,' and that's not the point at all. The whole reason to tour is to strive for something better. Forget about the costumes and staging, it's the music that counts. If you don't keep improving you're wasting your time.

I grabbed the guy's shirt. I wasn't going to let anyone get away with calling me a homosexual. But then John Reid intervened and the guy landed in a heap. We were whisked away by the police and they threw the book at John, when I'm sure they would rather have had *me* inside. *(The time in New Zealand when John Reid spent three weeks in jail for dealing with someone who made accusations against Elton.)*

When we got there *(Australia)*, we were invited to a reception by the Dean of Perth. We were so tired after the flight we rang him and asked if we could make it the next day. Fine. That night on RV there's a big story: 'Elton John snubs the Dean of Perth. He says he was in a mood.' Can you dig it? Everything is controversial, even Coronation Street. They have a sign flashing on the screen during the show – 'Not suitable for children'. They are so archaic, and they hate the English. Or at least the press hate us. We're still 'Limey bastards' to them. Since I found that out, I have willed every Australian team to lose. My cousin lives there and he had to accept the principles of a beer drinking idiot to survive. Don't worry, they already know what I think about them. When I go back they will be waiting for me. It was a nightmare being there.

I might end up like Elvis Presley hidden away behind iron gates. I have, the way I've become so elusive. It has reached the point where somebody has to go through about four people just to get hold of me.

Sport

I think I'd be a good Minister of Sport.

Watford FC

I've been a Watford supporter ever since I was a kid living
in Northwood. I used to get a Met Line tube to Watford, walk up
through the town to the game and stand at the Rookery End.
I've seen them in good times and bad times, and I'm not stopping
now. They made me a vice-president, but that wasn't enough.
If you want to help a club you have to spend money on it, and
to do that you have to be a full director.

I used to stand up on the terraces to see them. Once, I was beaten
up by some fans of the opposing team. And now I'm on the board.
I didn't ask to become a director. I thought they might think me too
pushy. But when they approached me I accepted like a flash.

When I first started getting involved with Watford, everyone thought
I was really crazy; then my mum and step-father got involved and they
realised that what I had with the club went much deeper. That it really
was a love affair. The day the club went down to the Fourth Division,
I was in New York. I rushed into this shop and used the phone to call
England and then, when I heard the result, I just sat on a chair and
wept. They must have thought I was mad!

Elton with Watford FC's Billy Jennings.

Elton training with Rod Stewart.

I'd be in seventh heaven if only I could be chairman of Watford football team! But I suppose I can't just go in and be chairman now. I don't know enough, for a start. But I'm sure I'll learn.

Most directors are stupid. All they do is put money in so they can bring their friends to sit in the directors' box.

Certain things go on in the game that I will not have Watford involved in. I thought the pop music business was corrupt, but the football business is head and shoulders above it.

Some players are asking for ridiculous tax free payments to join a club. It's very unfair. I don't get tax free money, nobody else does, so why should footballers?

I've never been so petrified in my life.
(After having drinks with the then England football manager, Don Revie.)

If I had to choose between still being at the top of the charts in five years and being chairman of Watford, I would choose to be chairman of Watford.

The other board members treat me well. Like a human being, not like a lunatic pop star.

Football taught me how to accept defeat with dignity. To listen to other people's point of view.

I'm not nearly as flamboyant as I used to be. I still enjoy being eccentric, but now I feel I have a responsibility to my team. I dress more soberly when I'm on duty.

I was forced to take on responsibilities which forced me to have self-confidence for the first time. All I had been getting before was gold albums.

The club has helped me tremendously because I've actually had to go out to the bank manager on my own or fix up accommodation for players. In the past I would always have had somebody to do that for me.

I got really excited the other day when I went abroad. I booked my own flight, got the plane on my own, took a taxi at the other end and checked into a hotel all by myself. A few years ago I would have had it all done for me and I thought here you are at the age of 31 and at last you can do it on your own, stupid sod. I'm flying back to Exeter the same day to see Watford playing football there, so I expect I'll arrive at the match with my head swathed in bandages.

That's dedication for you, isn't it? I get more nervous watching Watford play than I ever did when I was on stage.

You see I'm basically shy and running Watford means that I've tried to overcome this – I have to think a lot for myself and talk to people. I've been shy since I was a kid, but I always had a clearly defined goal and that was music.

I put back the starting time of my first concert in Glasgow on Saturday night so that I can watch the home game against Hull in the afternoon. I'll fly up to Scotland after the match. I am capable of being a rock'n'roll star and the chairman of Watford Football Club and I sell more records throughout the world than Rod Stewart. *(Replying to Rod's assertion 'he was probably born to be chairman of Watford Football Club and now he's beginning to look like the chairman of Watford Football Club'.)*

I'd never wear anything casual to a football match. When I go with my team to a game – and I go everywhere with them – I always wear a formal suit and tie. I wouldn't want to let them down. I'd hate anyone to say, 'There he goes, just another sloppy pop star, never wears a civilised suit'. I do it for tradition's sake. I respect that.

Elton with members of the Watford FC team.

I worry about losing Graham Taylor. Thankfully it has not arisen, if that came about I don't know what would happen. I am the sort of guy who lives life as it comes *(Taylor eventually left Watford for Aston Villa, and later became manager of England.)*

If someone had said to me that it would cost me £2.2 million in buying shares and making loans in order to achieve that dream *(Watford in the First Division)* I would probably have reached for my cheque book.

But you couldn't buy the pleasure I've had in being chairman. When I'm due to play in a charity game, I take it seriously, and go to Watford by train, but come lunch time and they all pack up and go home, or to the golf club, I go back in the afternoon and train with the youngsters.

When I'm finished with pop music, I still hope to be on the board at Watford, and I will always be fighting to bridge the gap between them and the fans.

It's OK to have your World Cup teams and all that... but Watford's where it's at for me.

I know I'm always going on about the club... yawn, bore, but it is terribly important to me as a person, it reminds me that I'm just a human being and brings me down to earth - literally!

I love going down to the club because being in rock'n'roll you never get a real chance to meet ordinary nice people.

It's a pretty time-consuming job and you can't be chairman and then only turn up at three matches a season.

I can see the day coming when I will stop playing music and make helping Watford a full-time job.

At Watford football club I even met girls flying over from America just to see me. They are very sweet but I've never slept with a fan. It would be very dangerous, very harmful, and it could totally louse up their lives. No way - it's unfair. But I've got myself in a position where I've got to be very careful about what I do. I'm responsible to a great many people, especially in my job as chairman of Watford Football Club. One has to be aware that if I recorded that kind of material *(referring to Wayne County's 'If You Don't Want To F-K Me, F-K Off')* I would upset a great many people in the town of Watford. On the other hand, as an artist I don't want to be forced to make such compromises.

I'm aware that people at the club look towards me for guidance.
I really enjoy that and I'm having such a good time that I never want
to ruin it.

What everyone has to realise is what those people have given me,
what they mean to me. They're the people who have kept me sane
through all this *(his football friends at Watford)*. It's why I would not
go and live in America when my accountants were telling me to.
I made the decision because of Watford and what I want to do.

I can't really play football. The only time I played a whole game
last season I broke my glasses in the second minute. I managed to score
two goals though – in fact I played much better without them.

Playing football and representing England in the international matches.
That would be true happiness.

On selling 90% of my interest in the club, I am pleased to have
been able to ensure the financial success of the club. I have spent
13 enjoyable years as chairman, now I'm delighted to be transferring
my shares.

Tennis

I'm a great tennis fan and I'm lucky to have seats for the fortnight
(Wimbledon). Once seated I have to stay there. Every time I leave my
seat I'm mobbed.

A couple of times I played with Jimmy *(Connors)* as my partner,
and every time I made a decent shot, he just sat on the grass and killed
himself laughing. It's a great game though, I just wish there were more
courts in this country.

If you can survive an hour long session *(of tennis)*, you know
you're in pretty good shape. I've got a gym at home, too, with the
usual sports equipment, like a cycle. That's not as interesting as squash,
but it does you a power of good! I need lots of energy for performing
and sport gives me that extra energy, and lots of fun into the bargain.

Elton with members of Vic Lewis's charity cricket XI.

I beat Billie Jean King at tennis once. I was standing there in a kind of daze when she came up and said 'Shall we play for real now?' And I thought 'Oh shut up'.

Billie Jean's *(King)* a really good friend of mine and she's a great lady. The thing I like most about her is that she'll fight and crusade for something she believes in, and she's done an awful lot for women's tennis. She's done a lot for my tennis too, and it's a real thrill to be able to say I've played a game with Billie Jean King. I take my racquets everywhere I go now, and if I have any spare time, I'm out on court. I love it. I remember once I was playing in a tennis final, and I got so annoyed with myself for not doing better, that I broke three racquets in the process! That's terrible, I know, but I'm very competitive.

Other Sports

Some people are born stars, others are born fans. Me? I'm a sports groupie.

I can't get into all the social thing of belonging to clubs – then having to book and only being allowed to play for so long and all the rest of it.

Sporting facilities for young people in England are a disgrace compared to any other country I've been to. Anyone who wants to win something for Britain has got to flog himself to death in his own backyard.

I hadn't played cricket since I was at school, and then I didn't play very much. Most of the matches were on Saturdays and Saturday was my day at the Academy of Music. It was either music or sport, and music won. Well, most of the time – in good weather I skived off occasionally. So when they rang me up to invite me to play in the benefit match I was quite chuffed. I tried to get some practice in but unfortunately didn't get much time. Still, I really enjoyed it. *(Elton played at Lords for the Vic Lewis Show Biz team against the Middlesex All Stars. He scored 24.)*

Musical Heroes, Friends & Enemies

John Lennon and The Beatles

I still think The Beatles were the be all and end all of pop music. What they did for pop music was incredible, unrepeatable. Of course there will be other musicians in the future who can maybe earn as much or even more money, make more records and sell more albums, play to more people at concerts... and so on and so on. But you can't take away what The Beatles contributed to pop music. They changed the entire scene. And it's because of them that most of us today are what we are. They were definitely my biggest influence.

John *(Lennon)* says he doesn't know how we do it, The Beatles act used to be 20 minutes and he says he used to think that was an hour. An eternity for him.

John *(Lennon)* said there were four of us and you do two and a half hours. I just couldn't have taken it.

I met *(John)* last year in Los Angeles briefly and we got on very well, and this year when I went to make the new album in New York I went to see him and he played me some rough mixes of 'Walls And Bridges' and he asked whether I'd like to do some 'oohs' and 'aaahs' and I said sure. I ended up doing piano and vocals with him, which was great. It was all done in about three or four hours. It was a lot of fun because he works really quickly. We've become very close. John loves New York. He can see the river from his place. He used to be on the Mersey and now he's overlooking the East River. With a mind like his, no way could he live in Los Angeles. The city is the place for him. And he's in a very productive frame of mind at the moment. (1974)

We did 'I Saw Her Standing There' which was great and I was so glad we did that. Originally I said, 'Let's do two numbers, but you'll have to do another. Why not do 'Imagine'?' He said, 'Oh no, boring. I've done it before. Let's do a rock and roll song. So I thought of 'I Saw Her Standing There' which was the first track on the first Beatles album. And he never sang it. It was McCartney who sang it. John was so knocked out because he'd never actually sung the lead

Elton with Eric Clapton.

before. For us it was very emotional and one rock paper crucified us. But it was just an emotional night and nobody could believe it. I knew John would be petrified about doing it, but he really enjoyed it. I was more scared than he was, hoping things would go right for him. But the reaction when he walked on stage... I wish he could have done more numbers because the reaction was so great. But he wanted to go upstairs and be sick. He told me he used to throw up before he went on stage.

For us it was very emotional (*performing with John Lennon*). I knew John would be petrified but he really enjoyed it. I was more scared than he was – hoping things would go right for him. He came to Boston to see us before we did New York and I'd never seen anyone so nervous in my life. He was so worried for us.

Top: Elton on stage with John Lennon at Madison Square Garden in New York on October 24, 1974. This was Lennon's last ever appearance before a live audience.

Bottom: Elton. Marc Bolan and Ringo Starr.

I couldn't believe it when I went to their New York apartment. Yoko has a refrigerated room for all her fur coats. And she has rooms full of those clothes racks like they have in Marks and Sparks. She makes me look ridiculous. I buy things in threes and fours. She buys fifty. The funny thing is that you rarely see her wearing them. She is always got up in some tatty old blouse.

The Beatles got ripped off for masses and masses. They were the innovators of the demand for a high royalty rate; a new group from Clapham want 50,000 dollars advance and they've got a good chance of getting it now, but that would never have happened then. Everyone's learned by their mistakes. They started Apple and we learnt from it.

The Rolling Stones

They're perfect *(The Stones)*. I mean Jagger is the perfect pop star, there's nobody more perfect than Jagger. He's rude, he's ugly, attractive, he's brilliant. The Stones are the perfect pop group, they've got it all tied up.

Somebody like Keith Richard is rock'n'roll through and through and I'm not like that.

Townshend's all right, but Pete's such a nice guy when you meet him. He's not like a Jagger. Jagger is an ego-maniac I'm sure but Townshend is down to earth. I thought he'd be an ego-maniac but he wasn't.... he was great. I mean, he has his moments when he'll be doing his thing for the people, but that's then. I played with The Who when I was in a semi-professional group and, oh God, they were arguing so much. He's controversial but there's nobody like Jagger... he's a bitch. He really is.

Rod Stewart

Rod Stewart was around even longer than I was before he made it. I can remember asking him for his autograph while I was still at school. I saw him and John Baldry at the Conservative Club, Kenton, when I was 17. Afterwards I went to the pub and went up to him and said 'Excuse me Mr Stewart. Can I have your autograph?' Wild! He used to come on stage with a scarf around his neck and sing 'Good Morning Little Schoolgirl'. I thought he was great. (1972)

He should stick to grave-digging, 'cos that's where he belongs, six feet under.

Rod was going to come tonight until he found out that it costs £250 for a table. Let's face it, that's what he has to pay for a hairdo. If you think I have trouble, his hair takes more work than thatching a Dorset cottage.

I was amazed Rod Stewart quit Britain because I remember going round his house to watch 'Land Of Hope And Glory' on his video machine - you know, the Last Night of the Proms. He said 'Doesn't it make you feel emotional?' and I said it didn't make me feel that inspired, so Rod gave me the biggest lecture in the world, and said, 'You can't leave England.' And then all of a sudden he went himself. It was strange.

Behind all the slagging we're great mates - a bit like Bob Hope and Bing Crosby. I'd love to do a Road film.

With Rod Stewart on stage at Watford.

David Bowie

I don't always retaliate when someone has a go. I didn't retaliate when Bowie said I was a token queen, even though he's had a couple of goes since. Because I know what's happened to him. I'll always remember going to dinner with him and Angie when he was Ziggy Stardust. It was a fabulous evening and over dinner he admitted to me that he always wanted to be Judy Garland and that's the God's honest truth.

Now I think the only guy that looks original is David Bowie – it's not overdone, and he's got a great taste.

I honestly think if he was working Bowie could have been... I think he is over here... on a level with what The Beatles and Elvis were. If he was still working there *(USA)* there would be terrible mob scenes but that's perhaps why he stopped working.

Queen and Freddie Mercury

I felt I missed Freddie that day, and I did *(the concert)* more as a tribute to Freddie than the AIDS thing. I didn't want to say anything about AIDS. I did it for my friend. I felt for the boys in Queen as well. People said 'You didn't go on for 'We Are The Champions'. But I felt that I didn't want to get involved in the bunfight. It was a very moving day and I enjoyed the audience's reaction, but I felt just kind of numbed by it. I was sad, and so my feelings were that I'd rather it was Freddie up there than me.

Elton with Brian May and Roger Taylor of Queen.

Others

Ringo Starr, Elton, Eric Clapton, Jeff Lynn,
Mark King and George Harrison on stage for
a Prince's Trust concert at Wembley Arena.

I didn't want to end up on the Los Angeles cabaret circuit the way
Elvis did. When I met him he looked like a tired old beached whale.
I looked into his eyes and there was nothing there - just a look of
vacancy where vitality had been. His flesh was tired and bloated.
He'd just become a puppet. I wish that someone had taken him off
the road and put him on a cure. I wish that someone had settled down
and had a word with him. When it comes down to it you can have all
the friends in the world, but the success and the quality of your life
depends on you.

Oh, I don't think I was ever in with the Hollywood set.
I met Groucho Marx and Mae West because they're legends.
Of course, there are several people in Hollywood that I like and that
are, well, Hollywoodish in their way. Diana Ross is one of them, and
an absolutely darling lady. And Cher, who is very mixed up but really
sweet. And Bette Midler... You know something? I always manage to
get mixed up with girl singers who are really the bane of everybody's
lives. Paranoiac plus. I'm very attracted to talented ladies like that.

Eric Clapton could come out in a dress and I wouldn't mind, as long
as he was carrying his guitar. I've always looked so ridiculous.

I'd like to write a song for Ray Charles because he's one of the
people I consider to be one of the all-time greats. I may be a disaster.
I may send him a song.

Groucho - he's just awe-inspiring for the first two meetings...
it's like meeting Mae West. Noël Coward's the only person that
I regretted never meeting.

I never get to see many concerts myself. But I went to see Alice Cooper in the States and it was incredible, with the helicopter, the shower of panties, the fireworks, it was the best produced show I've ever seen. Really amazing. I was caught up in it myself, scrambling for a pair of panties, and the band was so tight. You can't do that here, who's going to clean up the mess? But the scene is loosening up a bit.

I told George not to put it out *(his recording with George Michael, 'Don't Let The Sun Go Down On Me')* because I didn't think it was going to be a hit. I said to George, 'This is a very crucial time for you. You've had this album out *('Listen Without Prejudice')* which hasn't been as successful in the States as the 'Faith' album; maybe you should think twice about putting a live single out'. Then of course it was Number One in every country of the world...

Cook and Greenaway are the best commercial writers in the country and perhaps the world, although I wouldn't buy their records because that type of music doesn't appeal to me. I think they're a cut above McCauley and the others.

The artists who really rank at the top are Cohen, Jagger, Lennon, Zappa, Dylan, Simon and Garfunkel and - there's many more.

Elton with George Michael.

I had always been a Neil *(Sedaka)* fan. He has called me the most expensive publicist in the world!

When I listen to Carole King's voice now I have to just turn it off 'cause it sounds like they made 'Tapestry' twenty-five times and just cut eight tracks off it and put them on the new album. While me, poor sod, has been experimenting and trying to do something different. (1973).

Top: Elton with Neil Sedaka.

Below: With Bob Geldof.

He *(Bob Geldof)* came over to America thinking he was God's gift and that he was just going to repeat his success over here. He died a death. You've got to be prepared to work really hard here. He's just too big headed.

I admire Cliff *(Richard)* very much, as he's kept a hold on what he believes in and also makes very good music.

It's like I still have a thing for Dusty Springfield. I love Dusty. Whenever I meet her I think 'Jeepers, that's Dusty'. When I was living in that flat *(in Croxley Green)* I used to have 500 pictures of her stuck all over my bedroom wall. I would have to keep replacing them because when the winter damp came in they would peel off...
So you see I've still got my heroes and heroines. I may be a rock'n' roll singer myself, but I'm still a sucker for hero-worship.

He *('Legs' Larry Smith)* was the only person who kept me sane...
I get terribly bored when things are too serious. I want to get into funny things, so I might as well have a bit of comedy in my act.

They asked me to play on Jerry Lee's album *(Lewis)* but I said no. He was so disappointing when I saw him at the Palladium, and as far as I'm concerned, he was the best rock and roll pianist ever. I thought it was going to be a gas. I went in my drape jacket and got jeered at by the Teds. He could have wiped the audience out, but he just sat there and played country and western numbers as if to say – fuck you. All these old rock stars are the same. (1973)

I love The Eagles. They're the best band I've seen on stage the last couple of years. Rufus I really like, Joe Walsh – they're all favourites. (1975)

Of course he'll *(Chris Rea)* probably get a knighthood before me, anyway, because he isn't a poof.

One thing Ian Dury did really pissed me off. He had a go at me in one of the rock papers and stated, 'I don't wanna live in a big house like Elton John, I'm quite happy in catshit mansions'. Then the very next day in the Daily Mirror it read 'We went to interview Ian Dury in his new luxury hotel suite and he said he couldn't live in his place any more because he needed a good rest after his tour'. I thought, Ian, you hypocrite.

I don't believe Johnny Rotten isn't interested in money. I don't believe it. Johnny Rotten has claimed in the press that he was robbed but on the other hand he's not supposed to be interested in money and it's the money I'm speaking about.

When people like Generation X or Sham 69 have a go at me they don't stop to think that maybe I've bought their records.

His Own Band

I'll be perfectly frank, I'd never fired anybody in my life. Both members took it very hard. I did them both by phone. Nigel *(Olssen)* was in LA... he actually took it worse than Dee *(Murray)* to start with. But since then I've seen Nigel a lot and he's actually closer to me now than he's ever been. Even though underneath it all, he's still deeply hurt. Dee, however, is not talking to me. We've only had the one phone call. I phoned up and asked him out to dinner and he wouldn't go. He's a little hurt and I can understand that... It's an impossible sort of situation saying to someone after five years that they're out and that's it. But give it a little time and things will work out. *(The time EJ changed his band in 1975.)*

Elton with Princess Margaret and Tony Armstrong Jones.

Ray *(Cooper)* made an incredible difference to both the sound and the visual aspect of the group. He has given us exactly the new dimension we were looking for.

Princess Margaret was very knowledgeable *(about music)*. Apparently one of her favourite groups was Magna Carta, and Davey Johnstone used to play in that. Now he plays for me.